AF573623

MILESTONE SPORTS CARS

MILESTONE SPORTS CARS 1950 to 1965

Photos by ALBERTO MARTINEZ — Text by JEAN-LOUP NORY — Design & layout by JEAN-FRANÇOIS PUTHOD

ISBN 0 85429 386 8
A FOULIS Motoring Book
This edition first published 1983

Published by :
Haynes Publishing Group
Sparkford, Yeovil, Somerset BA22 7 JJ, England
Printed in France
by Berger-Levrault-Nancy.

CONTENTS

AC COBRA

A.C.COBRA 289

Only the bravest driver would ever try to control this British car — a hell-raiser on wheels. The A.C. Cobra of the years 1963-64 was one of the purest expressions ever of automobile brute force and speed. No doubt, you will be able to find your own words to describe this ferocious creation when you have read through the description in this chapter. Clearly, in what is after all, a book about production models, I shall not be talking about the 7-litre Racing Cobras with 480bhp and their giant struggles with Porsche and Ferrari or about the golden age of rally driving when courage counted for as much as the sheer power of the machine you were driving. That was the period when, every time a driver put his foot down along roads which were hardly wider than the racing Cobras themselves, he really did take his life in his hands.

Such a powerful brute was clearly beyond the capacity of the general run of drivers to control; even the best-known racing drivers had a real problem in getting the best out of the mighty engine, and sometimes even they could not tame it ...

But this is not the right place to get involved in a description of the 7-litre Racing Cobras, which were pure racing cars and could no more claim to be civilized than, say, Niagara Falls. I am here concerned with the more everyday beast. But even this was possessed of exceptional power: a small, 289 cubic-inch engine developing 300bhp DIN for a car weight of just 920 kg. Anyone with any automobile expertise will be able to grasp the significance of these figures: a power to weight ratio of 3:1 kg/bhp. For the most inexperienced driver, a quick way of ending up six feet under, and for one of even modest ability the need for some fairly hair-raising driving lessons!

In its earliest form, the AC Cobra had nothing at all of the powerful appearance of its sister racing Cobras. It was, in fact, the traditional all-British A.C., comparatively docile, straightforward, with normal tyres and lacking any element of the violent power which was later to so transform this entirely civilized and manageable car. The unleashing of that power was not long in happening, as we shall now see.

The original A.C. was equipped with a six-cylinder engine developing 127bhp SAE. It was a traditional car, with a steel body and a ladder-type chassis. Its only outstanding quality was that of independent suspension for all four wheels. During 1960, however, an American racing driver and instructor called Carroll Shelby took an old style A.C. and redesigned all its essential parts: thus was born the A.C. Cobra. But it was not to be until 1963 that the new car was completely ready — that is, equipped with all the characteristics seemingly designed to give any nervous passenger a heart attack.

The old straight-six disappeared, to be replaced by a compact V8 (Shelby was American) of 4727cc, with a 72·9mm stroke and a 101·6 mm bore. The aluminium cylinder heads were especially effective, producing a final compression ratio of II:I. This engine now gave more than 300bhp at 5750 revs, with the torque reaching 39·4mkg at 4500 revs. These simple figures should give the reader some impression of the power of this engine, which was equipped with four Holley carburettors. A cooling system of 14 litres completed the picture.

In addition to all the modifications described above, the old ladder-type chassis was completely discarded in favour of a tubular model — a very necessary modification to cope with 300bhp. A body of light alloy was then added to the chassis to complete the new Cobra, now prepared to eat up the road or track as quickly as any modern Porsche 3·3 Turbo! There was independent suspension front and rear by wishbones, coil springs and dampers (at first there was transverse leaf rear suspension). A bit old-fashioned, perhaps, but nevertheless the system was perfectly sound and quite capable of dealing with any unexpected movement on the part of a distracted driver. Although distraction was never part of driving the Cobra, which demanded total attention and lightning reflexes if one was to stay on the road. Even with Girling four-wheel disc brakes and crisp rack-and-pinion steering a few circuits of the racing track would still show just how frightening this car could be!

The dashboard was straightforward enough, with the instrument dials well displayed. A flick of the ignition key would now start the deep rumblings of the V8. Two or three touches on the accelerator and you would be up to 44mph in first, 87 in second, 125 in third — all this without pushing the engine and barely heating the cylinder block... I should perhaps add that this particular car is equipped with the four Weber twin carburettors which were usually peculiar to the racing 289s and which increase power to about 330bhp.

Let's see how the car behaves from a standing start. In first, you don't have to put your foot down to feel the wheelspin; in second, at 6000 revs, the driver needs all his concentration and energy for every micro-second to control the rear end of

The Cobra: an aluminium body, wire wheels and a bonnet thrusting out beyond the windscreen spoke of power and aggression.

The normal production carburettor was often replaced by four twin-choke Webers. This gave 330bhp from the 289 cubic inch engine and made a top speed of 150mph possible. There were disc brakes on all four wheels.

MICHELIN

Aggressive and tough in appearance, the Cobra was one of the most brutally powerful roadsters of postwar years. Opposite: the well equipped dashboard with its eight dials neatly grouped.

the car. In third, the engine is still uttering its characteristic bellowing sound, but the speedometer is now showing 110mph and, with strangely narrow tyres for the power, you will soon find everyone else on the road getting out of your erratic way to leave you room to pass. In fourth, the speed rises to 125mhp and there is still plenty of scope for more acceleration. But at this speed the driver of the Cobra can easily start to feel shivers down his spine; even when moving in a straight line, the car needs intense care in handling, although its road-holding is excellent. If you put really heavy pressure on the accelerator, you will get a very strong impression that the rear of the car is trying to get to the front. Flat out, the Cobra can reach a maximum speed of 150mph.

The tendency of the rear end to stray when the Cobra is subjected to rapid acceleration leaves little to the imagination as to what can happen in a bend if the 300bhp were suddenly fully deployed. Only the lightest possible touch on the accelerator is required, since the enormous power which the driver has at his disposal will punish the slightest error of judgement with a severity directly proportional to the seriousness of the mistake. When you know and feel the car intimately, you will also know when it is about to slide. The rack and pinion steering will not be at its most precise when taking bends, it is therefore very important, if not essential, to counter the impending slide by flicking the steering wheel in the opposite direction about one-tenth of a second before the rear end starts to slip. I have to confess, however, that 20 miles of fast driving in a Cobra reduced me to a state of jelly-like exhaustion; unless you are used to driving at around 125mph, the sudden flow of adrenalin leaves a very hollow feeling in the pit of the stomach.

Having said all this, the Cobra 289 remains a marvellous car, which only holds problems for people who are not used to it. The brakes are highly effective under any pressure and in any circumstances. Shifting from fourth to third is also very effective, and the resulting engine braking can easily push the driver's face against the windscreen as well as leaving two rubber slicks, 10 yards long, on the asphalt.

The gearbox too is very effective, the synchromesh working with a fine precision. At this level of power, there is little point in thinking about creature comforts: road-holding on bad surfaces is a much greater problem. Here, feather-like pressure on the accelerator is to be highly recommended, even if you have to look a complete fool by being passed by a Golf GTi at full speed. The Cobra was made for racing, for flat tarmac with good grip. On its own territory, you can let it have its head — elsewhere, beware!

Apart from the interesting handling, it is the bursts of acceleration of which the car is capable which are its most exciting feature. This particular car, developing 330bhp, can cover a standing 400 metres in 14·1 seconds — proving to an impressionable passenger that the driver is a real man...

2250DE92

ALFA ROMEO

SPRINT SPECIALE

Does the reader prefer white or black? For the writer, these two contrasting colours are both as attractive as each other. Similarly, I like the Sprint Veloce cabriolet just as much as the very attractive Sprint Speciale coupé.

The Sprint Speciale was a real jewel of a car. Even the empty body shell, in vermilion red, of this superb and rare Alfa-Romeo is enough for me. This little marvel of a car was led a quiet existence from 1957 to 1965. Quiet, because this model was a wild thoroughbred of car and therefore not highly popular.

Although it was developed mechanically from the Sprint Veloce, the Speciale or Alfa 'SS' was due to the genius of one particular designer, without whom this unique sports car would never have existed: Bertone. One of the most successful coachbuilders in the history of the art, with a unique eye for creating fine flowing lines.

None of the mechanical specifications of the Veloce were modified for the SS, not even the 225cm wheelbase, but the classical lines of the cabriolet, the work of Pininfarina, were completely remodelled, to produce a car of supreme elegance and beauty. However, in spite of its almost delicate appearance, the SS was capable of considerable speed and the design guaranteed great smoothness. Another remarkable aspect of the SS concerned its height: the Sprint Veloce cabriolet had a height of 1·26m, while that of the SS, in spite of appearances, was in fact only 1·24m. The beautiful lines of the car were rendered even more flowing by a large windscreen which sloped sharply and was very rounded. The effect was completed by a sloping of the roof from above the windscreen gently down to the rear bumpers and the sides of the car had a pronounced tumblehome. It is interesting to note that although Bertone made extensive use of rounded lines and curves, he was brilliant enough to resist the temptation of adding superfluous adornments to the radiator grille, bumpers or trimming, which a lesser designer might have done.

Unladen, the SS weighed 860kg, while the Sprint Veloce was slightly heavier at 865kg in the first version, which had a 1290cc engine. The specifications of the two models were obviously very close, except that the engine of the Veloce cabriolet only developed 90bhp, in contrast to the high-compression 100bhp DIN of the SS. This produced a differentiation in the power/weight ratio of 9·6kg/bhp against 8·6kg/bhp. It is worth noting the almost identical engine specifications, since acceleration and top speed differed considerably from one model to the other, those of the SS being markedly superior. The SS was capable of doing the standing kilometre in 33 seconds, or 2 seconds faster than the Veloce, and had a top speed of 118mph against 106 for the cabriolet. These differences in performance were due entirely to the more aerodynamic design of the SS, which reduced its drag to a minimum.

The model which we tried was not the 1300cc, but the 1600cc, which opened up even greater possibilities than the less powerful version. From 1957 to 1962, the small Alfa-Romeos powered by the 1300cc engine were called Giulietta. From 1963, with the appearance of the 1570cc, these models became known as Giulia. The basic version of the engine developed 106bhp, which was increased to 129bhp SAE (or 112bhp DIN) in 1965 both for the Veloce and the SS. This was still basically the same fine

Beneath the stylish lines of the 'SS' body was a twin cam engine giving 112bhp. Doors and other opening sections of the body were of aluminium.

The Sprint Speciale (SS) was designed by Bertone. A very low drag co-efficient allowed a speed of 125mph.

engine with twin overhead camshafts and two twin-choke carburettors. The compression ratio was 9·7:l.

There were no hidden mysteries in the gearbox. The five gears were all synchromesh, and perfectly designed to take full advantage of the power under the narrow bonnet. From 1957 to 1964 these cars were still equipped with four-wheel drum brakes, which had always been favoured by Alfa-Romeo. A year later, the change-over to discs was made in recognition of their undoubted superiority to drums.

I would, however, like to make one criticism of the SS, if I dare. Although the body was in most ways a delight to behold, it was heavy. The prototypes were completely made of aluminium, but production models had an all-steel body, except for aluminium bonnet covers, which hardly made any difference to the overall weight. The heaviness of the SS showed itself as soon as the wheels began to turn. In spite of exciting noises from the exhaust, the driver of the SS never had the impression that he was going to be thrown back into the boot as he accelerated. The rate of acceleration was, in reality, quite acceptable, but the dramatic shape of the body led one to expect even more. The smooth progression through the gears, and the action of the twin camshafts ensured a rapid enough take-off and 90mph could be showing on the speedometer even before you had had time to say goodbye to your secretary. The standing kilometre could be done in 31 seconds, an impressive achievement, and completely due to the car's aerodynamic qualities. The same level of performance could also be seen in the top speed of 130mph, which could be reached in a relatively short time. Even reckoning on an average 120mph top speed, the SS, powered by only a 1600cc engine developing 112bhp DIN, was still a high performance car. Its handling qualities, too, were a vast improvement on those of the Veloce, although the latter was just as powerful: strain flexing of the body was virtually eliminated and both ends of the car could be relied upon to behave themselves.

There were, however, a number of faults in the car, including the very soft suspension which, while making the ride very comfortable, made the body move about far too much. It was also a pity that the SS, with its very different looks from the other Giulia models, did not have its steering quality raised to the standard normally expected in a sports car. In some ways, it could be said that the SS flattered to deceive, and that it was not a real sports car at all, since it lacked the masculinity of cars truly of the genre. But this could also be taken as a compliment.

Other points of criticism? An over-large gearlever gate and brakes so weak they were liable to provoke a heart attack in any attempt to bring that beautiful body to a standstill.

In spite of the faults outlined above, which one should forget since such beauty should be unblemished, the SS remains one of those bewitching, truly good-natured cars which can turn the most ordinary driver into something of a poseur.

1600 SPIDER

In 1965, Alfa Romeo introduced no less than thirteen models divided between the Giulietta, Giulia and 2600 ranges. Included in these new models from the Milan factory (which also manufactured Renault Dauphines and 4Ls for the Italian market) were three drophead coupés: the Spider 2600, the Giulia Spider and the Giulia Veloce. The latter was a particularly attractive car, for two reasons. Firstly, it was very good-looking, with neat lines and an unaggressive front end. The attractive, gentle body-shape was a creation of the great Pininfarina and even a close examination of the car now will reveal hardly any jarring elements in the design which has an almost perennially fresh look about it. There is a feeling of classical restraint from the front bumper to the rear; every element seems exactly in place without the slightest note of extravagance — I hope that the readers of this book will agree with me. This attractive car, however is badly in need of revaluation since, in spite of its good looks, it is not much sought after by collectors.

It was not only looks, which made the Giulia an outstanding car, however attractive its beautifully proportioned curves may have been. There is no point in producing a car with a visually impressive body if the engine is too weak to propel it effectively. In fact, the Giulia Veloce was equipped with a superb four-cylinder engine, with twin overhead camshafts and twin Weber carburettors which gave, for the time, a very respectable 112bhp at 6500 revs. Behind the engine was a beautifully engineered, fully synchromesh five-speed gearbox. This, coupled with the outstanding agility of the car, made the Giulia capable of seeing off its rivals, which included at the time the Porsche 356 'C', the Sunbeam Alpine Series IV, the Triumph TR4 or even the Austin Healey 3000, even though the latter had a six-cylinder engine. The gentle looks of the Veloce effectively dis-

The 1600 Spider was an attractive car. This particular model is equipped with Campagnolo wheels which became available in the sixties.

3952R006

Right: the famous Alfa grille. Three dials monitor mechanical performance: the rev-counter is graduated up to 8000rpm! Opposite: the Spyder being driven down a palm-lined avenue — its natural environment.

3952RQ06

guised the power beneath the bonnet, but it was only necessary to exert a little pressure on the accelerator to dispel that slightly languorous look and to hurl the body forward in the conquest of its rivals. The Alfa was a very successful car, the more so since it was such a perfect combination of beauty and power.

The model which is illustrated in these pages is, however, even more special than the standard one described above. It has been carefully restored by Guy Gravier, its owner, and a number of substantial modifications carried out by the Italian specialist in tuned engines, Virgile Conrero. In this particular case, some extraordinary modifications have been introduced. Under the bonnet the 112bhp engine has been replaced by a unit developing 139bhp DIN at 6700rpm. This extra power has been achieved, not by adding a plethora of modified components, but by careful blueprinting work on the cylinder head, camshafts and the many moving components. The carburettors are two Weber 40 DCOE 2s. The exhaust system is the same as that of the GTA. In this way, 27 bhp has been added to the original specification without resorting to non-Alfa additions. The wheels were replaced by 14-inch Campagnolos (instead of 15-inch) with Michelin XAS 185 x 14 tyres.

The country behind Nice is mountainous; on winter days the sun shines palely over the rough landscape. The road is damp and, therefore, I set off quite slowly. There is no point, now, in using all the horsepower out of each bend. I take advantage of these first minutes to listen to the raucous noise from the exhaust, which becomes a really deep boom at 5000 revs. In front of the driver are the three main instrument dials, with the tachometer in the centre; I give myself a limit of 6000 revs, but the needle wanders over 7000 without any problem.

The rest of the instruments indicate that all is well with the engine: water temperature, oil pressure, voltage, etc. The driving position is excellent, with good back support. There is a bit of a problem with the pedals, however; the accelerator is too high to execute the heel-and-toe manœuvre satisfactorily, but one manages.

Taking the car up to its maximum in fifth, it hits an indicated 128mph twice, with the tachometer at 7200. The powerful engine is amazingly vibration-free and unstrained, even when pushed to its limits. In spite of the wind, the car doesn't deviate from a straight course. The pressure gauges remain steady. But as the roads become more mountainous, the Veloce begins to become slightly less easy to drive. In tight bends, for instance, the front end feels heavy and there is slight under-steer. But if the car is properly aligned, with the right pressure on the pedal, then any tendency to skid is perfectly controllable. Care has to be taken in fast bends, especially where the road surface is bad; in these circumstances, the back end tends to jump about a bit, although the fundamental stability of the car is still evident. Although the steering tends to be heavy in tight bends, it is otherwise very good and precise. The gearbox works smoothly, the pinions meshing with perfect precision. The gate, however, is too big and, coupled with the long gearlever, makes the movement needed to change gear longer than should be necessary. The brakes, disc front and drum rear, are efficient and powerful enough to halt the 960 kg of the car without any problem. However, the lack of power assistance is to be regretted, but there is no room for such a system under the bonnet.

With its engine developing almost 140bhp, this model certainly deserves the name of Veloce: plenty of power, but flexibility, too. In many ways, this very attractive drophead coupé (and not *spider,* as it was called by its maker) is the opposite of the British roadster of the same period in its streamlined design and ease of control, apart from the brake pedal. However, this is not to say that the stylishness of one is necessarily preferable to the more rugged character of the other. It takes different cars to satisfy different tastes.

Since the car described in these

The rakish lines of the 1600 Spyder were from the pencil of Pininfarina. Opposite: the amazing twin overhead camshaft engine left little room for non-essential accessories.

pages is a very special and rare models, I am now going to describe the principal characteristics of the *spider* Veloce in general production and available to the public in 1965. The engine was derived from that of the Giulia 1600TI. It was a straight-four, 78mm × 82mm, 1570cc unit with twin chain-driven camshafts — hardly the specification of a modern engine. The cylinder block and cylinder heads were in light alloy. The two carburettors were two stage Weber 46DCOE 14S, with air filters. At 4300 revs, the torque was 135mkg. All this points to a very sound car, and it should be remembered that the Italians were the kings of the 1600, twin camshaft, two-litre engine at that period.

ASTON MARTIN

ASTON DB 2/4

If one were to try to define the word 'nobility' in automobile terms, then the name of Aston Martin would inevitably spring to mind. The Aston Martin DB2/4 had all that indefinable distinction of the great period of the British sports car, when Triumph, Healey, Jaguar and Aston were the major names on the sports car racing circuits of the world. Although the DB2/4 now looks dated, it still gives the impression of being a well-built, aggressive car; the front end is squarish, while the rear, though quite elegantly styled, still has a very solid look about it. Glass area seems to have been skimped a little, but that is a minor point. The six-cylinder, twin ohc engine makes the DB2/4 a formidable rival to even the most modern cars.

Still a spirited car to drive, the Aston's main qualities are a sort of simple strength and an absence of major faults — even if there are a number of minor ones ... Getting into the driver's seat, for example. Without entering into an in-depth examination of the rationale of the relationship between the door-step, which is too high, the dash-board, which is too low, and the immense steering wheel, it is clear that the interior dimensions of the car leave a lot to be desired. However, after much leg-bending and trouser clutching (to make sure they don't get caught on the handbrake), it is usually possible for the driver to get into his seat with some concerted efforts.

Once in the seat, anyone — unless a member of an American basket-ball team — can find a perfectly comfortable driving position by adjusting the seat and steering wheel positions. This done, the driver can now feel at ease, although the steering wheel may be cutting into his knees; the gearlever, at least, comes easily to hand. Unfortunately, there is nothing on which the driver can rest his left foot, which gives the clutch pedal an unnecessary additional function. Another problem — due to the relative age of the car — is the non-synchromesh first gear, which could cause problems for a driver unacquainted with the car.

The main problems, however, lie in the ignition system, especially in city or other stop-start driving conditions, when the plugs tend to oil up quickly making the engine ragged. These problems, however, don't last very long once the car is on the open road, when the plugs clean themselves. And it is only on the open road that this car really shows its qualities. With its 2580cc engine (giving 127bhp at 5000rpm), the DB2/4 is capable of very high performance, although its speed and acceleration are limited by the car's weight (1250kg).

The slightly old-fashioned looks of the DB2/4 bely its capabilities. Its somewhat stiff, British style hides power which can still give a very good account of itself: at 5000rpm it can reach 31mph, 68mph in second, and 93mph in third — a perfect gradation. Once in fourth, 125mph is reached dead on 5000 revs. It is worth nothing here that the speedometer tends to err on the side of optimism, by about 10 percent and the instruments, in general, could have been laid out more satisfactorily.

When driving a left-hand-drive version, an oblique glance to the lower right allows the driver to read the rev-counter very easily. It is, however, very difficult to see the speedometer in the centre of the dashboard without some ocular acrobatics and virtually impossible to read the third dial, which includes the gauges for water temperature, petrol, ammeter and oil pressure. In fact, this dial can only be read from the passenger's seat, unless the driver takes unnecessary risks. Common sense would at least have dictated that it change position with the speedometer on left-hand-drive cars.

At 125mph the DB2/4 remains rock-steady, showing all its handling qualities, even in long bends. Inside, wind noise doesn't even interfere with conversation — all the more remarkable, since the model which we tried is almost twenty-eight years old. It seems, in contrast to the high interior noise in many modern cars, that the noise of the engine is left far behind in the wake of the car, leaving the occupants in peace.

The age of the car does become apparent on roads with broken surfaces, You don't have to be a specialist to guess the age of the suspension system, which is very hard — though not to the point of causing total dislocation of the human frame. The system is very much one of the 1950s, and very British, a quality I tend to admire, though this is not a view shared by everybody. Anyway, the lack of compliance in the suspension makes travel uncomfortable but not intolerable. At its date of manufacture, the system would have been acceptable for a sports car, but it certainly offers no more than the most basic level of comfort.

The DB2/4 can corner very quickly without any necessity for rapid corrections at the steering wheel. The rather heavy front end has a tendency to understeer in sharp bends, but a little throttle soon sets this right. At higher speeds any tendency of the rear end to slide soon corrects itself. All this is very admirable, the more so since these qualities are also evident on damp roads, when the road-holding of the car is quite amazingly

The Aston Martin DB2/4 with its familiar radiator grille. The forward opening bonnet allows a perfect view of the six-cylinder engine and the front suspension system.

7464-GZ78

Although the rounded form of this coupé betrays its age, the true quality of the DB2/4 could be gauged from its aggressive performance and also from the well-equipped dashboard, which had many small refinements.

TUDOR

7464-GZ78

7464
GZ78

K.P.H.
SMITHS
20 40 60 80 100 120 140 160 180 200 220 240
MADE IN ENGLAND
AMPS
30 30
RAD
FUEL
OIL
MADE IN ENGLAND

good. This is mainly due to the steering which is easy, precise and direct. The one reproach one can make is with regard to the immense size of the steering wheel which, even at the time of the model's introduction, must have looked as big as a ship's wheel! Perhaps is was simply intended as something for the driver to hold on to while taking fast bends, since the car was not equipped with bucket seats and the driver was therefore flung from right to left by centrifugal force. The front-seat passenger was fortunate indeed to have a special handle at his side to hang on to.

It would be very hard to find anything unfavourable to say about the brakes. In fact, there is nothing but praise for them; in no circumstances has it been possible to fault the performance of the four drums, even when tested to the extreme. A certain amount of effort is needed with the brake pedal, but such effort is entirely

in keeping with the discomforts of the hard suspension!

Aston Martin intended the DB2/4 for experienced drivers, at least experienced enough to appreciate the joys of the heel-and-toeing and extensive use of the gears. The car was certainly well enough built to stand up to such usage. The real enthusiast could also enjoy the double declutching necessary to pass from second to first! The perfect matching of ratios made the gearbox an exemplary piece of engineering, while the versatily of the six-cylinder engine made it possible to accelerate in fourth from as low a speed as 25mph. At that speed, in fourth, the rev-counter drops down to 1200rpm before climbing with astonishing ease.

Although it has its minor faults, such as the layout of the interior and restricted visibility, the DB2/4 2+2 coupé can still hold its own against most modern cars of medium capacity. In fact, it could probably have easily taken an increase in power, to enhance its other undoubted qualities. It is a shame that Aston Martin did not develop this model along those lines instead of turning to the production of even larger models which eventually had little to do with the classic sports car.

Right: the aggressive front end of the fifties Aston Martin. Opposite: ten years later the DB5 kept the same form of grille. The British dislike change!

ASTON DB 5

Until the 1950s, a so-called 'sports car' could, without modification, operate just as easily on the racing circuit as on the public highway. This was the golden era of the memorable battles at Le Mans between Morgan, Triumph TR3 and MGA, or between Jaguar, Mercedes or Aston Martin. During the following years, however, these high-powered, but essentially unpretentious car, began to disappear from the circuits to be replaced by much more sophisticated machines, specially developed for the race track. At the same time, the traditional sports car moved in the opposite direction, eventually becoming a much more comfortable machine, intended entirely for private road use and, in its more extreme forms, becoming essentially a 'grand touring' car.

Although not all sports cars developed in this way, by the mid-sixties most marques had succumbed to this fashion, including Aston Martin. The progression from one type of car to another is not hard to follow. Firstly, the weight is increased because the body becomes heavier, the chassis thickens and the interior becomes more luxurious. It should be said, though, that Aston Martin did try to maintain their contact with the racing circuits for some time, and there were some notable battles with Ferrari. But their production models were getting heavier all the time as additional comforts and refinements were added, in spite of one or two slimming-down operations, notably in the form of an aluminium body designed by Zagato.

In 1964, Aston Martin introduced a large coupé, or cabriolet, called the DB5. In spite of an aluminium body and a straight-six also of aluminium, this behemoth weighed almost 1500 kg. The adaptability and agility of past Aston Martins was finally lost. The latest model bearing that name was really intended to do nothing more than devour enormous distances along good straight roads and certainly not to pick its way nimbly around hairpin bends.

All this is not to say that the new, powerful DB5 was uninteresting. However, unlike the period of the DB2 and 3, when it was pure performance which counted, the new car expressed its quality in a balanced mixture of power, comfort and luxury. In other words, it was the perfect Grand Touring car and, if quality is one of the hallmarks of this type of car, then it can be said that the DB5 was one of the finest expressions of the *genre*. It was not for nothing that the DB5 was chosen in 1965 as the car to be driven

1782 QJ95

The engine of the DB5 was still a twin-cam straight-six, but now with three SU carburettors, giving 286bhp. The neat lines of the body were the work of David Brown and the Aston Martin factory. The well equipped dashboard was clearly that of a luxury car.

DAVID BROWN
ASTON MARTIN

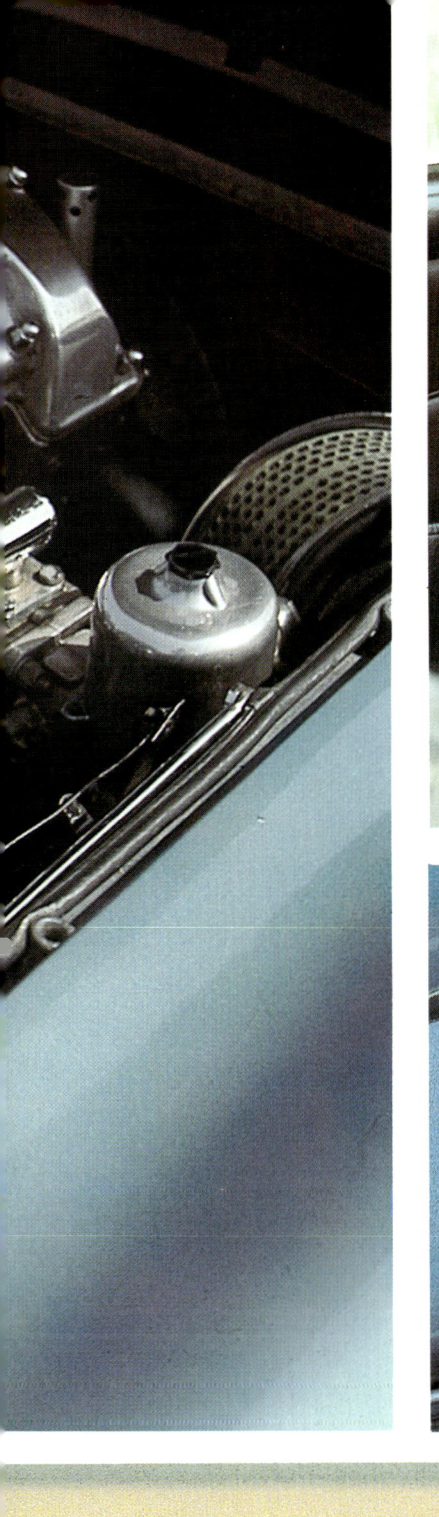

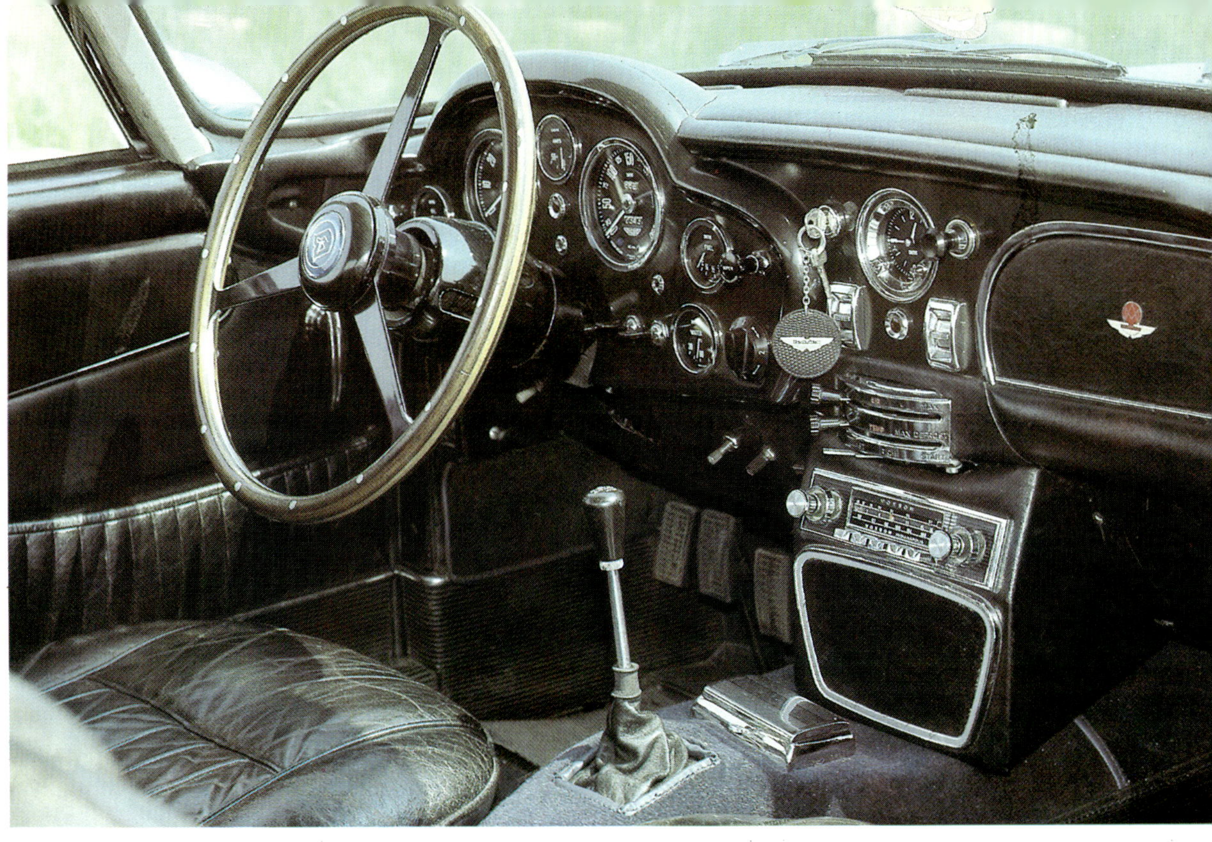

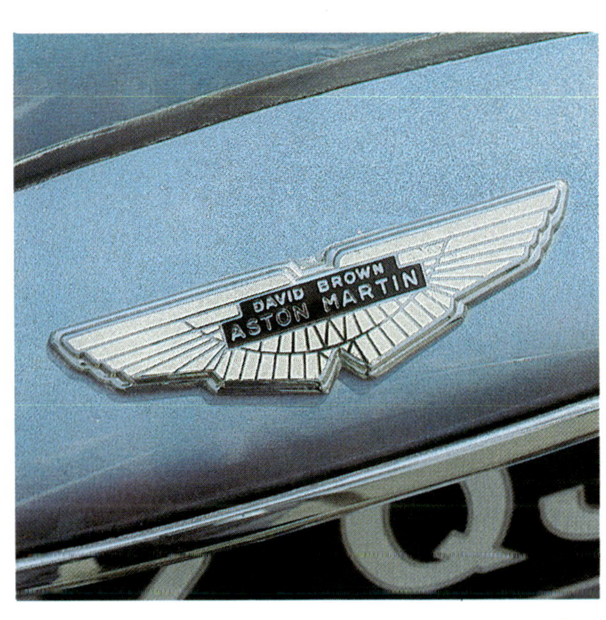

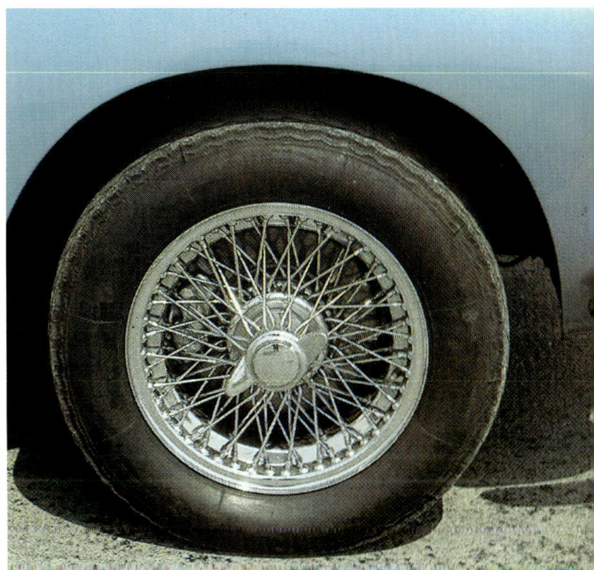

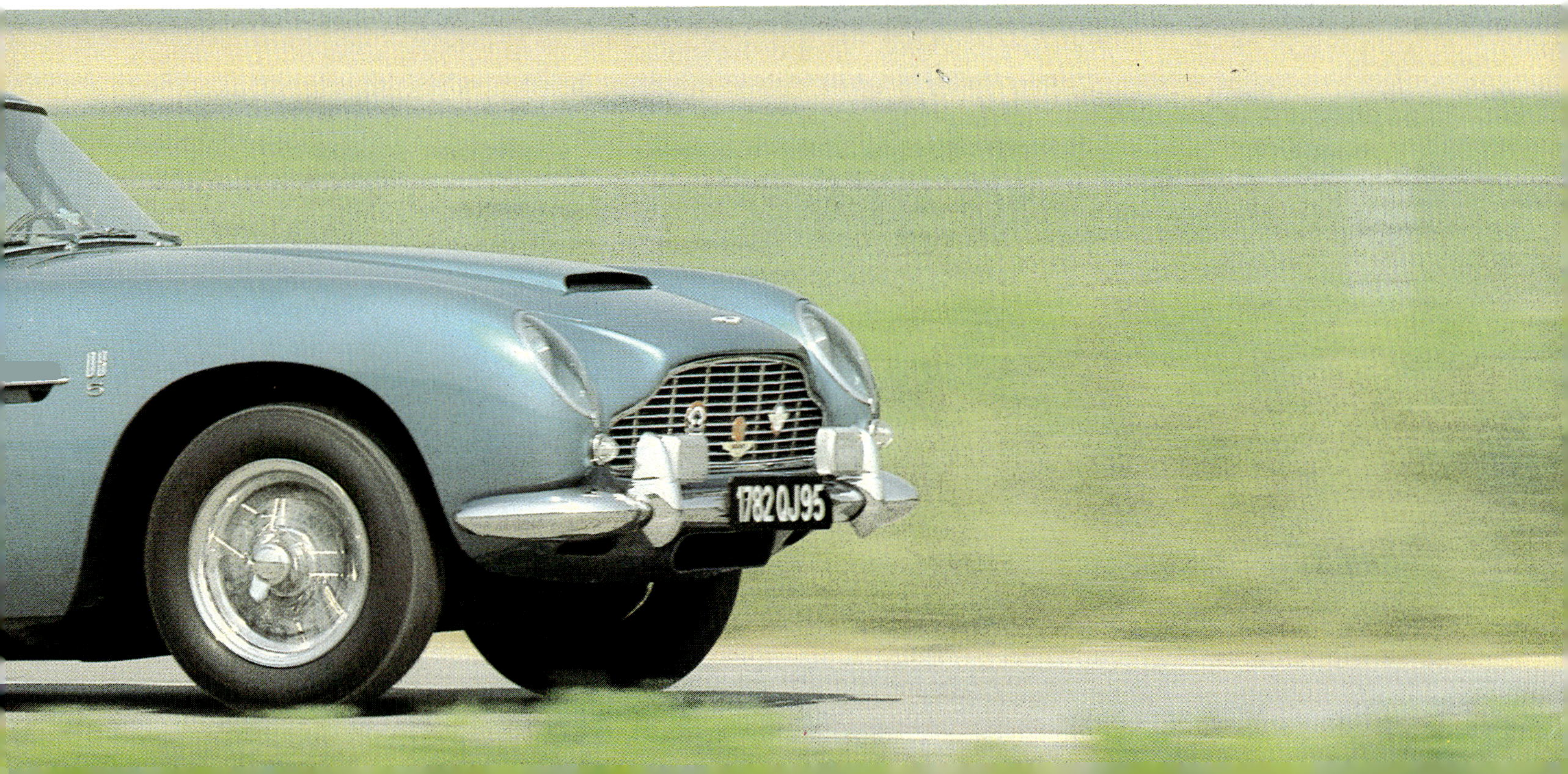
1782 QJ 95

by James Bond in the Bond films, fitted with the gadgetry and luxury fittings and all the wherewithall to impress members of the gentler sex, including an apparatus for dispensing three-pronged nails, a smoke screen, machine guns in the bumpers, bullet-proof windscreen, and so on. All this in addition to the powerhouse under the bonnet. Recently, though, 007 has been known to take on his enemies in a Citroën 2 CV. How the mighty are fallen!

In spite of its very generous proportions (2·49 m wheelbase and 4·57m length), the new model still looked very graceful, with a well designed front end, incorporating a small radiator grille and headlights streamlined into the wings. The only aspect which would lead me to disagree with the designers at Aston Martin would be the rear end, especially the way in which the wings came to a full stop with the rear lights, the only two sharp angles in a body which was otherwise all well-balanced curves. The body, made entirely of aluminium (rare at the time of the first introduction of the model) was designed at the Newport Pagnell factory of Aston Martin.

The chassis was a solid box-section platform type, strong enough to resist great torsional stress. In front, of course, was the enormous engine: a high-performance straight-six of 3995cc, 96 x 92 mm, with 80 degree overhead valves and twin chain-operated overhead camshafts. As I mentioned before, the cylinder block and heads were in aluminium. This very up-to-date design yielded the excellent figures of 286bhp at 5500rpm, while the torque was 39·8mkg at 3850rpm. The weight of the DB5 may very well have led one to expect a certain slowness in acceleration, but the 286bhp were well able to cope, placing this car in the premier position among fast luxury cars, with the respectable power/weight ratio of lbhp/5kg.

There was nothing remarkable about the fuel system, which incorporated three horizontal SU HD8 carburettors and two electric fuel pumps of the same make. The engine was water cooled, involving the use of 15·9 litres of water, the temperature of which was controlled by a thermostatic fan.

The transmission was more complex, since the owner could choose between several different systems. There was the four-speed version manufactured by Aston Martin itself, with a final drive ratio of 3·31:1, or 3·54:1. There was another four-speed version with overdrive, which was effectively a fifth gear with a final drive ratio of 3·77:1. The most popular version, however, incorporated a ZF five-speed, all-synchromesh box which worked very well and had a final drive ratio of 3·77 :1. There was also an optimal Borg-Warner automatic transmission with three forward speeds.

There was nothing remarkable about the suspension system, except that it was very well designed. The front suspension was independent by coil springs, wishbones and dampers, while the rear was by rigid axle, twin trailing links, Watts linkage, coil springs and dampers. The one outstanding feature was the hydraulic shock absorbers which could be controlled by a lever from the driver's seat. If it really worked, then this system was undeniably a fine piece of engineering.

There were Girling disc brakes to all four wheels with servo assistance. Steering was by rack and pinion.

With this impressive specification, the Aston Martin DB5 was obviously capable of very high performance: a top speed of around 150mph/240kmh and the standing kilometre in 28 seconds. This was not quite up to the figures for the equivalent Ferrari of the same period, but it was really the luxurious interior, the hand finish and the fine leather which expressed the essential spirit of the DB5.

From whatever angle the DB5 was viewed, it could hardly be faulted in its design. This was certainly one of the most successful models from the company.

1782 QJ95

185

AUSTIN

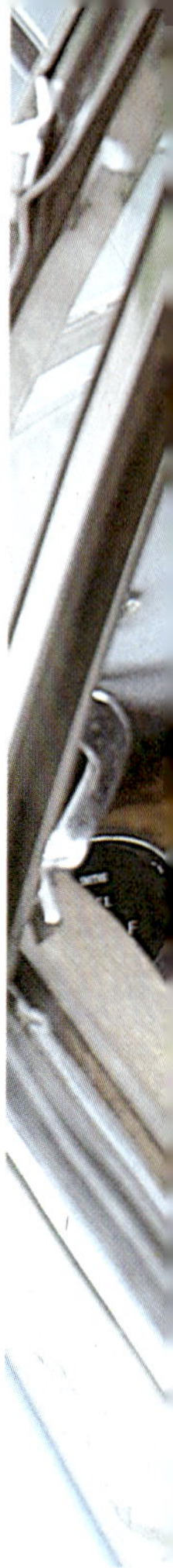

Fundamental in every way, the Austin Healey always retained a flavour of the traditional British sports car until its disappearance in 1968.

AUSTIN HEALEY 3000

The first car to be called an 'Austin Healey', the '100', was introduced in May 1953, and ended production in August 1956. The engine was a straight-four of 2660cc, developing 90bhp at 4000rpm. The 100 was available either with a three-speed manual gearbox (with overdrive) or a four-speed (100S). During its production period, 14,612 100s were produced. The 100-Six was introduced in 1956 and 14,436 units were produced from August 1956 to June 1959. As its name indicates, the new model was equipped with a straight-six of 2639cc. It came in two versions: the BN2 developing 102bhp at 4600rpm, and the more powerful BN6, with 117bhp at 5000rpm.

From July 1959 until April 1961, yet another model was made: the 3000 Mk I. It had the same body as the 100-Six, but there were very important mechanical changes. These included a straight-six of 2912cc and front dix brakes. The engine was rated at 124bhp.

The 3000 Mk II followed logically from the first version, and, from May 1961 to March 1962, Donald Healey brought out the BN7 and the BT7, both with new radiator grilles. The engines had the same cubic capacity as that of the Mk I, but three carburettors gave 132bhp at 4750rpm. No more than 11,563 of these models were made.

The 3000 Mk III was introduced in February 1964, and continued in production until January 1968. This was the last of the 'Big' Healeys. The MK III was the most powerful of all the models, developing 150bhp at 5250rpm. The interior was restyled to incorporate a wooden dashboard. This, then, was the car I tried out between two snow showers.

At this point, I should warn all motorsport enthusiasts who followed the fortunes of this make during the great period of the Liège-Sofia-Liège and the Coupe des Alpes rallies and other similar events, that the car driven by me here is not the competition model used in the 1960s by Timo Makihen, Tony Ambrose or Rauno Aaltonen. The cars used by those three champion drivers were very different from the production Mk IIIs. The competition models were given a 2968cc engine (instead of 2912cc) with cylinder block and heads entirely of light alloy. The compression ratio was changed from 9:I to 11:I, and with three Weber 45 DCOE carburettors, the engine then gave 200bhp. The usual body was replaced by one of light alloy, which gave these cars a performance far beyond the reach of the production models.

The interior appointments for both driver and passenger have been designed with only the minimum of ease and comfort in mind: narrow doors and low seats sandwiched between the doors and the transmission. In this model there are also two tiny seats at the back which could be useful for carrying extra passengers on a short journey. However, it is the driving position which is the most important: the dashboard includes a rev-counter and speedometer utilorated up to 137mph, with the petrol gauge to the left and then one of those curious dials, much favoured by British manufacturers, which includes water temperature and oil pressure. In the centre are the ignition, light and overdrive controls.

Beyond the windscreen lies the low yet ample hood, which is perfectly in keeping with the style of the car.

With the engine idling, the needle of the rev-counter hovers around 1000rpm. A little pressure on the accelerator brings a roar from the exhaust loud enough to split your eardrums. But at 2500rpm this noise disappears and the long, phallic bonnet leaps forward like a cannon ball. Not wishing to crash the car, I carefully keep to 5250rpm, maximum, on the secondary roads. At just over 65mph, at least I don't have the impression that I'm about to take off, though the noise, wind and vibration could easily give the impression that the car is travelling at 180mph.

I could hardly have chosen a worse moment to try this particular car. Now it's foggy and the windscreen wipers are useless... and the heating system has broken down. No point in worrying too much about these details, so I press on the accelerator pedal, which is so badly designed that it is very difficult to heel-and-toe with it, not just to frighten the rural population but because the gears are stiff and first has no synchromesh. In fact, I'd rather have a completely non-synchromesh box. First takes me to 37mph, then, very odd, second to 50mph, then a great gap, since third takes me to 75mph and fourth to 100mph. You then have to change into overdrive (which can also be operated in third) to crawl up to 112mph; at this point, the rev-counter is showing 5000rpm and I decide not to ask the car to do any more — it's too valuable. I certainly don't want to risk the big ends or con-rods. I have noted that the road-holding of the car is excellent, even on very bad surfaces.

The suspension (wishbones, coil springs and dampers in front; live axle,

The 3000 Mk III was recognizable by its grille and the four small lights beneath the headlamps.

semi-elliptic springs, radius arms and dampers at the rear) is neither too soft nor too hard, except perhaps at the rear. On French side roads, with their terrible surfaces which look as though they have been maintained with a hoe, the axle may occasionally transmit a powerful shock to the driver's backside, although this is somewhat softened by the padding of the seat. There is also some tendency to swerve, but this can be swiftly corrected with the easy, though rather less than precise, steering. Otherwise, this is a very fine car and it doesn't misbehave everytime the driver relaxes his attention a little. In fact, once I had got over my initial worries and learned to cope with some of its limitations, I began to find driving the 3000 a very pleasant experience. Its reactions are predictable, and there is something very friendly and comforting about the Austin Healey 3000.

These words are not just written for Healey enthusiasts; they are an exact record of my experience with the car. Another point in the car's favour are its brakes. Although they are mixed disc and drum, the servo-assistance is very effective and the car can be slowed amazingly quickly without any call for desperate pumping of the pedal or sliding of the rear end.

Whatever its qualities of endurance, the 3000 is a very pleasing car to drive, once the driver has got the hang of it. On the day on which I tried it, the only thing lacking was a ray of sunlight.

Obviously, the car does have its faults. It tends to overheat in traffic jams and really needs a supplementary cooling system. The weight of the totally outmoded cylinder block acts rather like a pendulum pulling the front of the car in tight bends. In fact, if you go too fast into a bend, you may find that the front of car refuses to respond to the steering wheel and continues straight ahead into a neighbouring field.

This is a type of car which is disappearing — intended to be driven by strong, silent men; smiling and smelling strongly of after-shave and who prefer slow deliberation to quicksilver agility.

LA GRANDE CASCADE

BENTLEY

CONTINENTAL

The description of a Bentley or Rolls is inevitably a very delicate matter. So great is the esteem in which this famous British marque is held that the slightest error is likely to bring all manner of criticism on the writer's head. This will be especially true of the car I want to describe here, since it is one of the greatest Bentleys ever built and any inaccuracy would therefore be doubly punished.

The car in question is a Bentley Continental, although it is a later model than the first ones which came out in 1951 with styling reminiscent of the Buick Riviera of 1950. The introduction of the Continental was an event of considerable significance at the time. The mechanical specifications made the new Bentley a sports car, at least in performance. It was capable of reaching a top speed of 120mhp, thanks to its 4566cc, six-cylinder engine and its reasonable weight of 1700kg, made possible by the large amount of light-alloy in its construction.

The model which we tested is not the purists' car, since it dates from 1959, when the styling had already been slightly redesigned. Nevertheless, the unforgettable radiator grille is still there. The roof still slopes as gracefully as ever towards the rear end, which remains just as pleasing to the eye with the rounded wings neatly enclosing the boot lid. It is the way in which the grace of the rear harmonizes so well with the aggressive front end which might lead one to talk of "perfection" in describing this car. In comparison with earlier models, the wheels are now completely exposed, which I find a distinct improvement. In all, I rather prefer the 1959 version of this distinguished car.

In contrast to the Bentley Saloon, the Continental was given all-aluminium coachwork, which concealed a lot of very high performance engineering. The engine was, of course, the six-cylinder 4887cc, with a lot of hidden power (probably it would not be unreasonable to reckon this at 150-160bhp in real terms). Fuel feed was by twin SU HD8 carburettors with sliding pistons and automatic chokes. This classic engine had a compression ratio of 8:l.

The gearbox was even more attractive, being the Rolls-Royce automatic with four forward gears, like that used in American cars of the same period. Fourth could be engaged direct (l/l), while the final drive ratio was 2·92:l (3·42:l for the saloon). The rear axle was rigid with semi-elliptical springs and links limiting torsional stress during braking. Front suspension was independent with springs and anti-roll bar. The brakes were servo-assisted drums. The one drawback to the model described here was the steering, which was not power-assisted and took 4 1/2 turns from lock-to-lock. Power steering reduced this to 4 turns on models so equipped. The tyres were 8·20 x 15. The fuel tank held 18 gallons.

The slightly curved dashboard incorporated all the usual instruments and numerous additional gadgets almost lost in the solid walnut. These included the button to control the hardness of the shock-absorbers, a small chrome control in the centre of the steering wheel which could reverse the function of the horn control with that of the headlamp main beam control. Another innovation involved the conversion of the petrol gauge into the oil gauge simply by turning a knob. The filler cap could be controlled electrically from the dashboard and, by the driver's left foot, was a button to control the headlights and a second one for the horn. The windscreen wipers were two-speed and were also equipped with a windscreen-washer. A final refinement were the armrests on the doors, the height of which could be adjusted.

The driver, then, lacks nothing as he sits at the steering wheel. This would hardly be the car in which to drive up to the snack-bar of a motorway service area. The Continental was really a sort of marvellous plaything. In the first few miles in the car, the driver is bound to be struck by the size of the steering wheel. Changing down presents no problems, except to lead to a certain unsteadiness on some very bad roads. The lack of noise and the level of comfort are quite extraordinary, although there is some wind noise from the windows which have started to move very slightly. From the engine, though, there isn't even a whisper.

The ideal cruising speed of the Continental is about 75mph, with the rev-counter at 2500rpm. The danger zone on the counter starts at just 4250rpm, and a lot of effort is needed to get the car up to 112mph. The comfort cannot be faulted, the easy suspension and the padded leather seats really do give the occupants the impression of floating on air. The body tends to sway on rough surfaces and heel over in bends, but there is very little disturbance to the interior calm of the Continental.

Handling is a problem, since the Continental does not take tight bends easily and, if the bend is long, then the body sways about and there are difficulties staying on line until speed and use of the accelerator come to the rescue. Partly, this problem comes from the gear ratio.

The rear seat of the Continental, heavily padded and covered in thick leather and with plenty of room for the passengers.

First takes us up to 25mph, second to 50mph and third to 78, which means that, to get the maximum out of the car, the automatic transmission has to be used as though it were manual or the kick-down has to be used to get all the power at the right moment.

Although the Continental was thought of as a very sporting car at the time of its introduction, it would now not be reckoned more than a large luxury saloon. Indeed, very high speed is not recommended, the steering is too imprecise and the brakes are only just sufficient to bring the car to a halt in normal circumstances and could certainly not be trusted to stand up long to hard use. The engine characteristics and gear ratios made this the ideal car for country drives or long journeys by motorway in absolute silence.

In addition to the multitude of dials set into the rare wood fascia, the dashboard of the Bentley also included a folding shelf. A massive and bluff front end in contrast to the sweeping lines of the rear.

CASCADE

BMW

Right: the old-fashioned and Spartan looking dashboard of the 507, with its strange steering wheel which was rather like those of American cars of the same period. Below: the safety belts. Without its hood, the 507 could look quite elegant.

BMW 507

The lines of the BMW 507 somehow expressed a sense of power, but power diluted by a certain grace and gentleness. This mixture contained the apparent aggression of the 507 and also indicated real breeding. The lines of the bonnet stretched forward, to drop suddenly and end in a discreet radiator grille before being wrapped round underneath the body, merging into the lines of the wings. This stylistic device somehow managed to convey, admirably, both the sensitivity and the brute force of the car. Another memorable feature of the trim was the raised chrome band running along the wings from just above the front wheels almost to the door handles, thus highlighting the classically elegant shape of the wings.

generous pockets, was of real leather. Unfortunately, the seats themselves, though obviously made to look and feel good, were not especially well-designed and could not hold the body in bends. The driving position was perfectly acceptable, but in certain positions the spokes of the steering wheel could obscure the oil pressure gauge or the thermometer, according to the wheel's position. But only a very slight movement of the head was necessary to correct this.

Like all V8s worth their salt, the engine of the 507 made so little noise when idling as to be almost sepulchral. The only sound to be heard was a slight murmur from the two exhausts. But once the necessary pressure was applied to the accelerator, the murmur would disappear to be replaced by a grumbling, and then all hell would be let loose. Yet, at the same time, acceleration was very smooth. The gearlever was cantilevered towards the left, but came very easily to

Although the BMW 507 was introduced more than 25 years ago, its fine, pure lines have made it remarkably resistant to changes in fashion, the principal external indication of its age being the large, narrow wheels (600 × 16). The fuel tank held 60 litres, while the total weight was 1250kg.

The dashboard was of simple design, but included a full range of instruments. Two large dials indicated speed and revs, while the rest of the panel was taken up with various knobs. The horn control was located in the hub of the steering wheel and the headlight main beam control in the wheel's circumference.

Thick carpeting and high quality leather characterised the fine finish of the 507. Even the inside door trim, with its

hand. The synchromesh was usually reliable, but it was sometimes quite hard to move the gearlever from one gear to the next. The first two ratios were satisfactory enough, but third was too "short" and did not make up for the engine's unwillingness to rev. Even when fourth was engaged, the needle of the rev-counter could still hover for a very long time around the 4000rpm mark. With a little patience, however, it would gradually creep up to 5000rpm, at which point the maximum power of 150bhp would be reached. The speed would then be a round 125mph, or the 118mph claimed by the factory.

At this point, the car we were trying held the road very well. We reached this speed with the hood down, so it should

Leather trimmed door with side pockets. Opposite: the 507 at speed.

be remembered that a certain amount of drag would have been created. The hard-top version was capable of reaching a speed of 130mph. The performance, then, was acceptable but not brilliant; acceleration suffered badly from the relatively heavy weight of the car and the lack of power. No one would ever describe the 507 as a record-breaker nor any serious driver expect rapid acceleration through the gears. Indeed, the 507 always felt as though it was thinking about something else.

Even in first and second gears at low revs the rate of acceleration was much too low. Below 3500-4000rpm there seemed to be no real power at all and the engine felt very dead. For that reason a lot of use has to be made of the gears in heavy traffic conditions to keep things moving. If the road is long and twisting, with a hairpin to the right followed by a long bend, it is much better to find a ratio to hold the car in balance. In these, conditions, road-holding was noticeably less sure and the equilibrium of the car needed constant attention, especially since the rear end had a tendency to stray because of the suspension by rigid axle. Road-holding was not dramatically bad, but the driver had to take all the necessary precautions. In damp conditions this became absolutely necessary. Yet in spite of these criticisms — no agility and imperfect road-holding — the 507 possessed certain much more attractive attributes which could, in certain circumstances, put the driver into ecstasy.

Steering was extremely easy, and positively invited the use of opposite lock. In fact, with its directness, precision and ease, it could well have served on cars much more powerful and built to much higher specifications.

There is very little to be said about the braking system, except that it tended to bring the car to a halt very suddenly after slowing it down. The car which we tried was equipped with front disc brakes (an option at the time of production) and these performed admirably. There was no question, either, about the comfort of the car, largely due to the compliant suspension system. The torsion bars gave the 507 a suppleness which would have been very acceptable in a grand tourer.

The 507, then, had very little of the real sports car and could, perhaps, be considered more of a GT model in disguise. The engine noise sounded quite convincing and the steering was perfect, but its road-holding was really only suitable for a lovers' tour round the countryside. This lack of true sports car performance is to be regretted, since the looks of the car promised so much, but its graceful lines did not hide anything more brutal. However, the 507 will continue to give a lot of pleasure to those who love it.

BRISTOL

BRISTOL 403

The Bristol 403 was a British car. Or, rather, almost British. I say 'almost British', since Bristol, originally an aeroplane manufacturer, made an agreement before World War II with the German company BMW to jointly develop a commercially viable sports car. In fact, the Bristol was very much a development of the old BMW 328 of 1938 and, twenty years later, was easily recognizable as such, at least externally.

The familiar double vertical grille, for example, reappeared on the Bristol 403 of 1954, although the wing grills of the engine compartment of the old BMW had now disappeared. The rear end also had certain BMW family resemblances, with the sudden slope of the roof down to the tail, which was tapered and flattened.

In spite of the obvious likeness to the pre-war German cars, the engineers of the Bristol Car Division did make some attempt to incorporate distinctly contemporary design features, including all curved surfaces and with never a sharp edge in sight. The old-fashioned look of the car was entirely due to the narrow radiator grille and the two-part windscreen, which had not been seen for several years on many American cars.

The general style, then, was British, and perhaps the most interesting aspect of the 403 was the engine. Derived directly from the BMW power unit, it was a straight-six of 1971cc (66 x 96mm). It was hardly the most modern of engines, but it did include pushrods and overhead valves, the latter being inclined in a V-form. There was also a pressure oil filter and an oil cooler to allow sustained high performance. The maximum power was a comfortable 101bhp at 5000rpm; maximum torques was 14·8kg at 3500rpm, which hardly raised high expectations for rapid acceleration from lower engine speeds. Bristol enthusiasts will know that fuel feed was by three Solex carburettors, and that, as was usual at the time, the fuel pump was, unfortunately, mechanical.

If my description of the Bristol up to this point gives the impression of an averagely attractive car with solid but unexciting mechanical parts, then some of the more unorthodox features hidden beneath the bodywork will come as something of a surprise. The chassis was made up of box members, which gave reasonable rigidity. But the suspension systems were an unusual mixture of components. In front, the suspension was independent by transverse leaf-spring, an amazingly antiquated system to find in a car of the time. At the rear was a rigid axle and torsion bars, the whole being stabilized by four Newton telescopic shock absorbers: these at least were in keeping with the time. The brakes were hydraulic with four non-assisted drums. Among this extraordinary array of mechanisms, only the rack and pinion steering (three turns lock-to-lock) conferred a note of modernism on the Bristol so that it did not lose touch completely with the more sporting cars of the time: after all the Bristol 403 had certain pretensions to being a high performance car, although with touches of quite considerable comfort.

The seats were well upholstered and would not have been out of place in a limousine; the hybrid suspension systems seem to have served their purpose and gave a reasonably comfortable ride. Other points in favour of the 403 were its relatively light weight (1225kg unladen), its ample engine power and the light, precise steering. Against it could be reckoned its price and its rather stuffy looks which hardly suggested a serious rival to other contemporary drophead coupés.

The Bristol Aeroplane Co. Ltd. was perfectly capable of making planes to fly, but what can be said of its motor car operation? The 403 itself was long (4·90m in overall length) and was therefore hardly ideal for mountain roads. The dashboard was neatly designed behind a large steering wheel; the instrumentation was very complete but possibly a little disorganized. Above it, the driver could see — with some difficulty — through the small windscreen the long bonnet stretching out before him. The steering was easy and sensitive at all times, but the gearbox was a fourspeed with 10 synchromesh on first gear, which hardly went with the sporting pretensions of the car and was more suited to times when the roads were much less crowded than they had become in the 1950s. In addition, the ratio spacing of the forward gears left a lot to be desired. There was a massive gap between first and second; hardly the best arrangement to get the car quickly and effectively through winding roads. Top speed was about 102mph. It should be remembered, though, that the top speed took a very long time to reach and that once the engine had passed 4200/4400rpm, it gave the rather disagreable sensation that it didn't want to rev any more, a characteristic in keeping with its long stroke.

Despite the astonishing suspension system, road-holding was good and predictable, at least on well-kept road surfaces: classic understeer at first but, if the car came into a bend very fast, oversteer, but without any real danger thanks to the

It is hard not to like the rather strangely styled Bristol 403 with its rounded back and the front, which so resemble the BMW 328. The spokes of the steering wheel look rather like cattle horns. This was still a car to be reckoned with.

precise steering. However, an additional 20bhp would have been very welcome to balance the car on the throttle.

With a top speed of over 100mph, and reasonable acceleration, this curiously obsolete hybrid could still combine the roles of luxury saloon and sports car at the beginning of the fifties. I fact, I believe that the Bristol was more luxurious than it was sporting, and it was a fundamental error on the part of the manufacturers to try to include both qualities in the same car. Its suspension was unacceptable even at the time: a more modern system would have turned the 403 into an acceptable luxury car with sporting tendencies, and not the reverse. Everything in this car seems to have been conceived backwards.

BUGATTI
BE

BUGATTI

BUGATTI 101 C

The fame of Ettore Bugatti really began in 1924 with the success of the supercharged Type 35 in Grand Prix races. The thirties were golden years of exceptional activity for the company at Molsheim, during which they produced a number of outstanding cars, including the marvellous Bugatti Type 57. The business was run by Ettore, the father, while the manufacturing and mechanical sides were looked after by Jean, the son. The latter was killed while testing a Royale in 1939, and Ettore died in 1947.

The story of the Bugatti marque after World War II is certainly much less interesting than in the years of Ettore and Jean. In 1951, Roland Bugatti, Jean's brother, decided to bring out a car with a modern body design by Gangloff, but under which was hidden a chassis dating from 1934! The new car was very long (5·20m) and the chassis was still sold separately from the handbuilt body; the engine design was already seventeen years old... The reasons for such an error in marketing are not hard to find: the company was virtually without capital; Roland knew nothing about the motor industry and the great Bugatti family lived in the past and had little enough grasp of present conditions let alone plans for the future.

The 101 C was an eccentric car, composed effectively of the Bugatti Type 57 chassis, designed in 1934, and modern bodywork by Gangloff of Colmar. The new design appeared in 1951 and was very classical, with long, pure lines. The radiator retained the famous horse-shoe-shape of the marque and there were wire wheels and a two-part wind-screen. The least successful part of the design was the rear end where the boot had oddly rounded edges, strongly reminiscent of the years 1936-40. More serious, however, was the fact that the overall proportions were all wrong, no matter how attractive the immense bonnet and the prominent, stylish wings with their suggestion of thirties design, looked, the overall impression of this huge car was still somewhat freakish. Looked at from the side it was still possible to admire and like it; the first three-quarters of the car would pass any visual test; but the back was ugly and insipid.

It is hard to blame Gangloff for the shortcomings of the design. He did what he could with a long wheelbase (3·30m); he managed to keep the famous Bugatti bonnet, give the car four good wheels and stylishly finish the four seats in leather. The dashboard was very complete, with two big dials and all the necessary small ones. The straight-eight engine, though, was now extremely dated, even with its two overhead camshafts. If you know anything about the supercharged Bugatti Type 57 there is no point in reading what follows, since everything was identical in the 101 C engine, except for the camshaft drive which was now by chain and not pinions. This was the most significant innovation, but was not enough to give the new car much help.

The all-steel body weighed 750kg, but the chassis was another 1000kg! There was still a very powerful engine to drive the 1750kg, to which it was necessary to add the weight of 100 litres of petrol. Once the supercharger was working, the engine gave 188bhp at 5200rpm; unsupercharged, the engine developed 135bhp at 5500rpm. The old-fashioned power unit was a straight-eight of 3257cc with a 72mm bore and 100mm stroke. It had two overhead

The profile of the Bugatti 101 C emphasises its length. The door visible just behind the right front wheel concealed the spare wheel compartment.

camshafts and its one-piece crankshaft ran in six plain bearings. Fuel feed was by a Weber 36 DCF carburettor and the supercharger. The engine was further equipped with a mechanical fuel pump and a Bugatti oil filter for a sump with 15 litres capacity. As everyone knows, the electrical equipment was by Scintilla. The compression ratio was 6·5:l, and the torque 27mkg at 4200rpm.

When the model was first introduced, the customer could choose between two gearboxes: a manual four-speed with non-synchromesh first, or the Cotal electromagnetic box which also had four speeds but was extremely silent and smooth. The chassis and suspension systems, however, were very unsatisfactory. The chassis being made up of enormous side members held together by cross-members of the same size. However, perhaps the most extraordinary feature of the supercharged 101 was the two rigid axles. The front axle in nickel-plated steel through which passed the leaf springs was classic Bugatti ... but in 1951-52 it was so old-fashioned as to be absolutely unique. The front springs were semi-elliptic with an anti-roll bar, and the rear springs reversed quarter-elliptics. The system was completed by Allinquant shock-absorbers.

After the Paris motor show of 1938 the Bugatti 57 had been equipped with Lockheed dual-circuit hydraulic brakes, which became one of the most up-to-date features of the 101 and 101 C. But even this and the steering system, with its worm and nut mechanism, could not rescue this amazing assembly of obsolete engineering from its eventual fate.

This, then, was the specification of the 101, the last Bugatti and a car intended to revive the postwar fortunes of the company. The outcome of the introduction of the 101 was complete and utter disaster. Only six or seven models (there is disagreement on the exact figure) were actually made, either in limousine or saloon versions or as the four-seater cabriolet which was the standard 'works' design. It was in one of the latter that we drove a considerable number of miles along the roads of the Bavarian forest.

The large door opens and gives convenient access. The seats are big and deep behind an immense steering wheel, though with plenty of clearance. The turning circle is closer to that of a lorry than a car and the heaviness of the steering makes turning the wheel the equivalent of weightlifting; in all, a nightmarish experience! The sound from the 3·3-litre Bugatti engine is deep and strong, introducing a sporting note. Once pressure is applied to the accelerator, the performance of the 101 is perfectly creditable and the car moves forward responsively and with a certain majesty. When all the power is unleashed, including the supercharger, the massive weight of the car is pushed forwoard without any problem. Clearly, there is nothing very exciting about the rate of acceleration, but the way in which the 101 attains speed is very respectable. It is not difficult to reach 100mph and the engine still remains flexible at that speed. There is no sideways movement nor indecision in the steering.

It is difficult to comment on the relative comfort of the 101, or on the working of the suspension system or the handling, since the Bavarian roads are in excellent condition. The unfortunate shortcomings of the rigid axles are thus minimized, except over joints in the road surface or on level crossings, when the occupants of the car are shaken in all directions. But the well padded seats are so comfortable that they absorb much of the potential discomfort being thrust up from beneath the car. Another agreeable feature of this 101 is the Cotal gearbox which is gentle and docile: a loyal and willing servant. The gears can be charged with just finger pressure without declutching, but the system does tend to overheat.

The four large alloy drum brakes are inadequate, especially at speed. In fact, the pressure needed to operate the brake pedal spoils much of the pleasure of driving the car. Why the system was never designed to be power-assisted we shall probably never know.

Similar criticism can be made of the steering. This is so imprecise, directionless and hard that it is rather like turning the handle of an empty coffee grinder. In tight bends the heaviness reaches such a point that the driver feels that he is moving a huge block of concrete along the road. But it is hard to see how this could have been otherwise, given the exceptionally heavy front end and the archaic suspension and steering systems. In longer, easier bends, the impression of not being able to turn the steering wheel is much reduced, but then the driver has very little idea of what the rear end is doing, since it tends to hold the road very badly.

The only way to drive the 101 C is with a certain dignity. Although it is fast, responsive and comfortable, it certainly cannot be treated like an overgrown sports car, no matter the past glories of the marque it may trail behind it. No, the last of the Bugattis is not a car to be treated roughly as an everyday car; it remains a reminder of times when motoring could be pursued with a greater sense of dignity than is the case nowadays or even when it was created in the early fifties.

The engine of the 101 C was basically the same as that of the supercharged 57 designed in 1934. The gearbox was an electromagnetic Cotal with four forward speeds. Even with its hood up, the lines of the 101 C were still elegant.

MAIRIE
DELAHAYE
345 BCJ 7·5

DELAHAYE

The body of the Delahaye 235 was designed by the young Philippe Charbonneaux. Well secured, the spare wheel took up virtually the whole of the boot. The steering wheel with its sprung spokes; on the left is the tiny gearlever for the Cotal gearbox.

DELAHAYE 235

It is worth looking briefly at the history of this make before examining the 235 in greater detail. The legendary years of Delahaye were before World War II, in the thirties, when the quality of their sports cars ensured a series of victories on the track and in endurance trials and rallies. After the war, however, the marque seemed to lose impetus, as well as having very little capital for investment. The traditional French coach-builders seemed to lack inspiration and tended to produce overblown, overweight bodies which covered out-of-date engines and massive chassis.

Compared with the international competition, the large French sports car was living in the past. The sports car renaissance of the postwar years was led by the Italians and the British. Ferrari had seriously introduced the twin overhead camshaft engine, while Jaguar and Aston Martin had streamlined the bodies of their cars to such an extent that speeds of 125mph were easily attainable and the standing kilometre had become a matter of 30 seconds.

In contrast, the French sports car designers were floundering in the past, with such models as the Bugatti 101 and the Delahaye 235. It was time for the French to bow gracefully out of the market before the performances and claims of their sports cars were seen to be totally ludicrous. The mistake made by Delahaye was to represent the 235 both as a grand touring car and a sports car at the same time.

The 235, with a modern body by the young designer Philippe Charbonneaux, weighed just over 1·5 tons. For all its massive weight, the car was only equipped with a relatively small 3·5-litre engine, with single camshaft and an iron cylinder block and heads which was so heavy it might easily have tested the strength of a World War I tank on the Western Front. There were three Solex carburettors which contributed to giving the whole antiquated assembly 152bhp at 4200rpm.

However hard the drivers of the 235 tried to wind their vehicles up to performances worthy of the car's supposed position, they certainly had no need to use their horns to clear a way for themselves on the highway. This said, however, we have done the standing kilometre in 36 seconds with a gearbox which tended to slip slightly; the trials held by the magazine *La Vie Automobile* produced 35 seconds with a car in perfect condition, which would be very good for a modern 1300cc engine in a middleweight car. The top speed was a respectable at 113mph. The only problem was that it took an eternity for the engine to yield its maximum performance; it can be safely said that there was nothing exciting in the performance of these six cylinders!

This power, or lack of it, was transmitted via a Cotal gearbox, which comprised three epicyclic gears, one of which was mechanical and other two electro-magnetic. This gearbox was very easy to manipulate: the driver simply took the forward gearlever (or the reverse lever), put the starter (located near the steering wheel) into first and then declutched. There was then no real need for declutching to move from one gear to another, up or down, since this function could be carried out by the electro-magnets. Obviously, the driver could use the clutch if he so wished, but there would be little point in not using one of the few positive features offered by the 235. There were, however, two disadvantages craftily hidden in this ingenious mechanism: the first was a tendency to give off too much heat, and the second was a very 'short' second gear ratio. First took the car up to 44mph, while the second gave up at 62mph — this was the problem — and

The rear end design of the Delahaye 235 was typical of the fifties, but this photograph shows how the design has aged.

the third took the speed up to 93mph. These speeds were obtained at 3500rpm.

The suspension system was nothing exceptional: independent with leaf spring at the front, rigid axle and semi-elliptic springs at the rear. The real surprise of the 235, however, was in the braking system, which I discovered to my cost while trying the car on the slippery roads of Champagne. As I have said, the rate of acceleration is hardly going to push the occupants of the car back into their seats, and I therefore decided to handle the car very much within its capabilities. The six cylinders started to work effectively at about 700rpm which gives 25mph in fourth without any problem, the kilometre coming up in 39·8 seconds. Given the great weight and the modest specification of the 235, this was quite satisfactory.

We were holding a straight course along the road when we hit a series of bends — nothing very serious, but still needing fairly energetic braking. I press on the pedal, but nothing happens — It's times like these that I wish I had never got into the car in question! I grip the steering wheel and devote all my energies to obtaining some response from the brake pedal and quickly drop down two gears. (One of the great paradoxes of this huge saloon-in-disguise is that heel and toeing is possible). Barely helped by the braking of the engine, the 235 finally starts to slow down. The truth of the matter is that the brakes are cable and the wheels lock one at a time. This system means that the effort of braking is raised to epic proportions. I have said elsewhere that the 300 5L and the XK 120 had inadequate braking systems, but in comparison with the total ineffectiveness of the 235 brakes they were quite acceptable ....

The steering also demanded considerable effort, both physical and mental, especially in tight bends, where the drain on the strength of the driver really becomes appreciable, reaching its most intense in hairpin bends taken at speed. It is a pity that the unsatisfactory steering and brakes urge the driver to extreme caution, since the handling of the 235 is perfectly reliable. There is the usual understeer in tight bends, neutral in long bends and oversteer it needed. Any tendency of the rear end to move off line can easily be corrected, thanks to relative precision and directness of the steering, which has few faults. However, when the 235 is at a standstill, the steering becomes immovable. This is no exaggeration; indeed, so stiff does the wheel become, that one is afraid of breaking something in trying to budge it, but, in contrast, it immediately becomes very easy as soon as the car gathers a little speed.

The instrumentation on the dashboard is satisfactorily complete, with rev-counter, pressure gauges and so on. I have no criticism to make of the driving position, except for one detail: the bad positioning of the windscreen wipers. The 235 can hold four people in comfort in its spacious interior. The boot is on the same scale as the rest of the car and there is also a complete tool kit to go with the rest of the luxury specification.

Since the car was obviously designed for grand tourism rather than sport, I had expected a more obviously luxurious interior, but in fact comfort does not go much deeper than surface appearance. The 235 can be very tiring, especially on bad roads, where the unsatisfactory suspension is more obvious. Although the Delahaye 235 was not quite the total failure which has sometimes been suggested, it did not measure up to its pretensions or its competitors. However, it will undoubtedly always be remembered as one of the only French representatives of this type of car from its period.

FACEL VEGA

The aesthetic evolution between the HK 500 and the HK II, which appeared in 1962. The latter model was more refined in every aspect, including the rear lights (below).

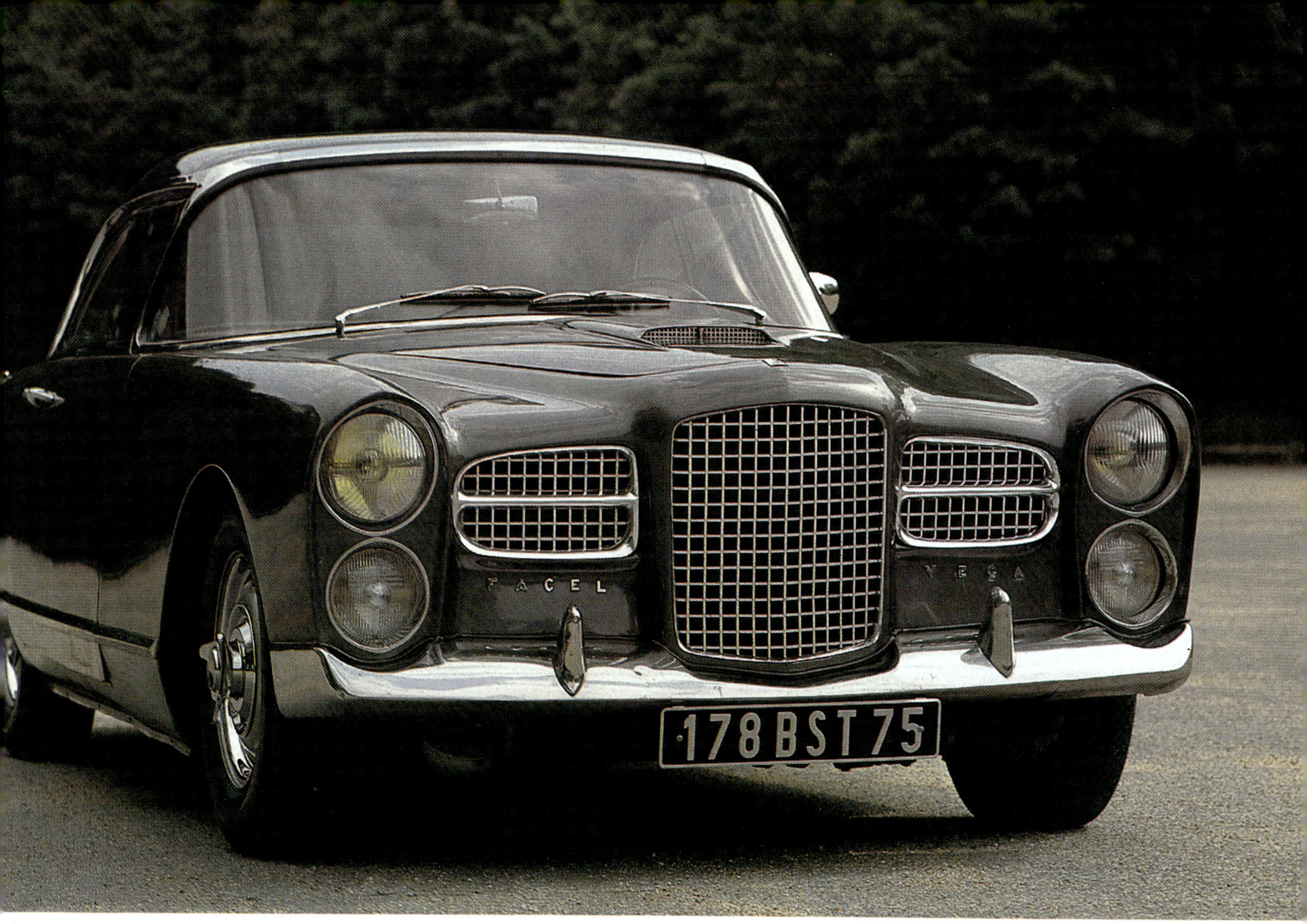
FACEL
VEGA
178 BST 75

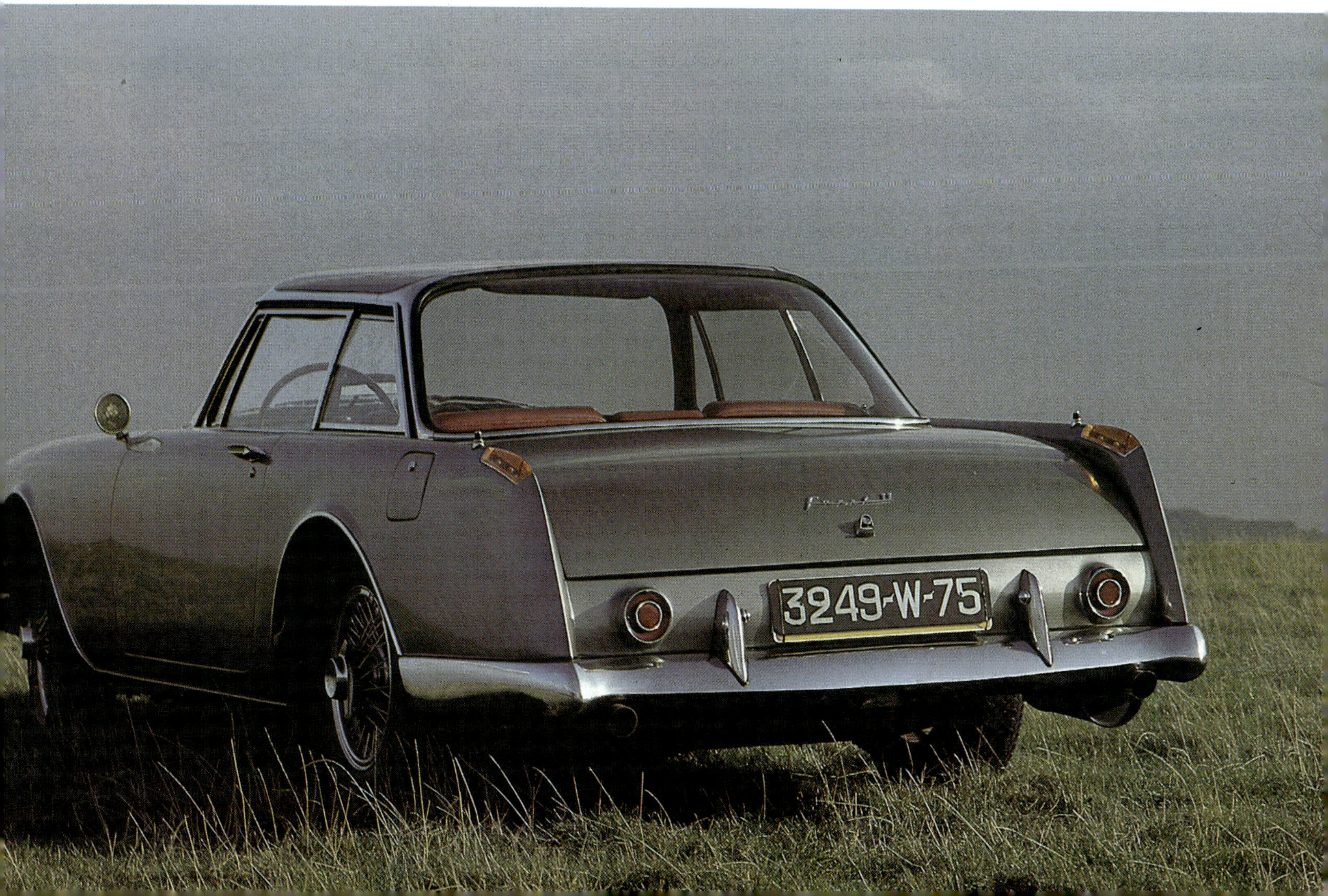
3249-W-75

FACEL HK II

The 1961 *Salon de l'Automobile* in Paris saw the appearance of the Facel II, with its simple lines, discreet radiator grille and a beautifully sloping windscreen. Gone were the heavy, bloated lines of the fifties with their armour of chrome and their high, curved roofs. The purity of design of the new version of this grand tourer was incontestable, although it retained much of the style and charm of the earlier model. Nowadays only the problems of handling so much size and power on narrow roads will reveal the car's descent.

The purists and critics did not hesitate to express their views of the new model, especially of its hybrid character: an American engine — a Chrysler Typhoon of 6·3-litres — a ridiculous suspension system, a French gearbox and British disc brakes. All this was unforgivable for those who wished to preserve the purity of the French car industry. And the final criticism was the price, which was considerable for the period.

Such carping can now be forgotten in favour of a more objective examination. So, twenty-two years after its first appearance, I finally tested what I regard to be the most beautiful French car ever (and one which will probably occupy that position for a long time yet). A few statistics will reveal immediately what area of performance the car occupied: 0 to 100kph in 9·2 seconds and 0 to 200kph in 32·6 seconds. At maximum revs (5400) the standing kilometre became a matter of a mere 30 seconds, with the car reaching 113 mph on the speedometer. Its detractors will undoubtedly point out that the Facel II was equipped with a 6·3-litre V8 giving 383bhp and that its performance is therefore not especially impressive.

They would, however, be forced to admit, that there were very few cars which could measure up to the Facel at the time, and certainly not at its weight of 1700kg. Only the Ferrari 250GT, the Aston Martin DB4 and the 300SL Mercedes could be regarded as being in the same class. It should be noted that the Facel II driven by us was not pushed to its absolute limits, because this was not really possible in the circumstances and also out of respect for the car. Nevertheless these performance figures do remain outstanding, especially since some of the technical specifications still left a lot to be desired.

The rear suspension was by semi-elliptic springs, but there was no anti-roll bar and no radius arms to minimise the movement of the rigid axle. I therefore expected a ride which would have more in common with flying an aircraft through turbulent air than riding on firm ground.

In fact, the Facel II was, in this respect, a pleasant surprise. Long motorway bends could be taken at 140mph without driving the occupants to prayer; almost flat out round the bend, and the car would still hold the road well. On inferior surfaces, however, the car would become much harder to control and even fairly moderate bends taken at 95-100mph would need very careful attention. In these conditions the body started to roll and the nearside rear wheel would finish by bearing virtually none of the car's weight at all. The rear end would then start to move about and the place where it achieved stability again would depend very much on the dips and bumps on the road surface.

In compensation, though, the massive power of the V8 totally cancelled out any tendency to understeer in tight bends; a touch on the accelerator and the rear would take off, the Facel passing out of the bend without a problem. However, a more precise steering assembly would have been preferable, especially if the car

is to be taken to the upper limits of its performance. The steering was quite direct, but had a certain imprecision. The car which we tested was equipped with power steering which, although generally found in non-sports luxury cars, was an advantage in this particular case. In fact, I must confess to a certain weakness for this solution, since it makes the turning of the wheel when the car is stationary or moving very slowly so much easier, unlike the classic systems which would have made driving the Facel rather like driving a 1920s truck.

This luxurious car was almost beyond criticism. Its fine profile was dominated by the immense windscreen and the steeply sloping rear window. Under the bonnet was an American 6·3-litre V8.

3249-W-75

FERRARI

FERRARI 250 GT

It is often claimed by doctors that there is a cure for most every illnesses. In certain cases, though, it proves impossible to get rid of all the traces, however good the cure. Testing any Ferrari, even one twenty-two years old, is enough to infect you with 'Ferrari fever'; once contracted, traces of this illness will linger forever. A Ferrari is like a strong drug; it is almost impossible to be cured of the addiction.

Everything about the car combines to seduce even the most reluctant driver. To begin, there is the light feeling of the aluminium door. There are the pure lines, still as elegant today; the fine Borrani wire wheels with their 600 X 16 tyres. Altogether, the Berlinetta weighed only 960 kilos — the same weight as a modern Renault 5 Turbo — any comparison, however, would cease there. The powerful light-alloy Ferrari V12 developed 280bhp at 7000rpm. Added to this was a four-speed syncromesh gearbox, rear-wheel-drive and very efficient disc brakes on all four wheels.

Perhaps there would be nothing especially exciting in this description of the Ferrari, if it were not for the 280bhp. It is certain, however, that the passenger seat was not intended for anyone easily frightened. The Berlinetta was strictly a twoseater with two good, real sixties-style bucket seats with adjustable backs which held the occupants firmly in place. To the left of the driver was an enormous rev-counter, marked up to 8000rpm, but with no danger zone! The speedometer was to the right and reflected the car's power since it was graduated up to 300kph (186mph). In the centre of the dashboard were five other dials: oil pressure, oil temperature, water temperature, fuel level and clock. The two main dials, however, say a lot about the capabilities of the Berlinetta — capabilities which would make it very hard for the driver's eyes to remain for long on the dashboard!

The sound of the V12 is enough to excite even the most stolid. Even murmuring in a traffic jam it is still a memorable noise, something to be taken in and reflected upon carefully. In fourth, we can drop down to 38mph; then we can start to hear the sound really open up as the engine flexes its muscles.

The driver begins to get the feel of this extraordinary car as the speedometer reaches (125mph) at 5500rpm. Above 4500rpm the noise from the engine becomes terrible, but even at 125mph the throttle pedal has not finished its travel. The rev-counter gradually climbs from 6000 to 6500 and in a few seconds the speedometer needle is quivering on 150mph. As the speed rises, and the road rushes beneath the car. The engine still seems to be asking the driver to go faster. At high speed the Berlinetta holds the road extremely well, even in a high cross-wind. When I drove one at speed, however, I did have time to notice one thing: it was impossible to take a hand off the steering wheel to sound the horn, which was controlled from the wheel hub. The main headlight control was also very hard to operate. On my right, it seemed that the other cars on the road had come to a complete standstill, while the roadside armco barrier had now lost all recognizable form and had become a shapeless streak following the route of the Ferrari.

At the maximum speed of 168mph the rev-counter settles at 7300rpm and bends approach at an alarming rate. However, in spite of the damp road

surface, the Berlinetta holds the road firmly, although this road surface is extremely good. I do notice that when it is less good — for instance, where there are expansion joints — then either the front or rear end may move about quite sharply.

The perfect cruising speed seems to be about 150mph. What most impressed me at maximum speed were the brakes, which seemed to exert extraordinary power in slowing down the car's 960kg. The servo-assistance works immediately, and even braking 155mph, to avoid a car changing lanes, caused no skidding. At the relatively venerable automobile age of twenty-two, the Ferrari 250GT could still compare favourably with a Miura or a Ferrari BB. It is indeed one of the most remarkable cars of the postwar era.

Its acceleration made it the 'Concorde' of sports cars; 0 to 100kph took precisely 5·2 seconds; 0 to 200, 17·8 seconds. With careful clutch work, the standing kilometre was a matter of

The Ferrari Berlinetta 250 GT was the perfect combination of virile power and beauty; this was really a racing car in disguise and was capable of 168mph.

A speedometer marked up to 300kph (186mph) and a rev-counter up to 8000rpm! Beneath the bonnet was a 280bhp V12, to propel the 1000kg car. Right: the huge petrol filler cap, which has had a padlock fitted here to deter vandals.

The Spider California adopted most of the layout of the 250 GT. However, the body was now no longer entirely of aluminium (only doors, bonnet and boot lid) and the engine developed only 240bhp.

—SPIDER CALIFORNIA

The choice between driving a Scaglietti Berlinetta (960 kilos/280bhp) and a Spider California (only 240bhp) would be almost impossible to make. If anyone were asked which they would like to try first, then perhaps the most sensible answer would be 'The one closest to the door'.

In spite of having 40bhp less than the Berlinetta, the Spider California was mechanically an almost exact copy of the more powerful car. The engine was basically the same 60-degree V12 of 2953cc, with a bore of 73mm and a rather short stroke of 58·8mm. Although the cylinder block was the same, the heads were less highly developed and changes were made to the camshafts, which explains the slight drop in power to 240bhp at 7000rpm. Maximum torque was 26·7mkg at 5000rpm, while that of the Berlinetta was 28mkg: a very small difference obtainable at 5500rpm. These differences made the engine of the Spider more tractable, capable of idling quietly in town at 2000rpm and then rapidly, but smoothly, moving up in performance. Fuel feed was via three Weber DCL 36 carburettors with electric pumps.

The gearbox was the classic four speed unit, with Porsche-type synchromesh and a single-plate clutch by Fichtel and Sachs. Rear suspension was by live axle, radius rods, half-elliptic leaf springs and dampers; the front was independent by wishbones, coil springs, dampers and anti-roll bar. The whole system was solid and straighforward, without any over-elaboration or complication. In this it was typical of the time. Typical, too, was the fact that it was equipped with four Dunlop servo-assisted disc brakes, although this was one of the least satisfactory features of the Spider, but only because of a softness in the pedal action. The brakes themselves were very efficient indeed — so powerful, in fact, that over-eager application could easily bring the driver's head into violent contact with the windscreen.

The Borrani wire wheels of the test car were equipped with 175 × 16 tyres, which detracted considerably from the power of the brakes. Similarly, road-holding was less than satisfactory, but the use of such tyres clearly pin-points the constant arguments between purists and those of us with slightly more practical ends in mind. For those who want every car to be in its absolutely original state, it doesn't matter if the vehicle is equipped with bicycle tyres, as long as they are authentic, even if this gives road-holding qualities well below the real capacity of the car. I must confess that I tend to support the view that there is no harm at all in fitting more modern, high-performance tyres, in spite of the cries of outrage from the purists calling it a mis-representation of history. I certainly prefer to drive a car which has been re-equipped in this way. Bends can be taken much more quickly and the full power of the engine can then be brought into play. Braking is no longer a hazardous series of crab-like jumps, with the car eventually coming to a standstill yards beyond where this was originally intended to happen, simply because the tyres were not of a high enough quality to react properly.

All this is, of course, a question of personal principles and philosophy. Although I happen to hold one point of view, I can still respect the other, since it clearly means a great deal to its adherents. The Spider California which I tested, then, was equipped with tyres of a design dating from the time of its introduction.

The stylish and elegant profile ot this marvellous car hid its brute force well. Streamlined headlamps, and the power of a fabulous V12.

6508

Even employing only two-thirds of the power available, the car became really hard to drive. Using the accelerator became much more than a simple reflex action; it was more a question of bringing a surgical precision to this relatively simple operation. The effort of driving the Spider may therefore be imagined; it was like conducting to Battle of Trafalgar in a wash-basin.

Although the chassis of the Spider was multi-tubular, like that of the 250 Berlinetta, the body was no longer entirely of aluminium. Only the opening parts, such as the bonnet and boot covers and doors were of light alloy. The rest of the body was steel. The weight of the Spider was therefore somewhat greater (about 1100 kilos), in spite of having the short wheelbase version of the chassis. Cars having the shorter chassis (240cm/94·5in) were recognizable by the air intake on the bonnet and different rear end styling.

The performance of the Spider, with its smaller engine and heavier body, did not quite approach the raw energy of the Scaglietti Berlinetta 250. This was a less serious, open-air car, made for modest country drives at 125mph. In fact, of course, the Spider was still and extremely powerful and fast car and one which demanded great care in its driving.

Before climbing into the Spyder and taking the wheel, it is well worth making a close inspection of the near-perfect lines of the car. In fact, it would be very hard to find one word of criticism to level at the external features of this dream car, before trying out what lies hidden beneath. The lines are pure and simple, down to the headlamps under their streamlined covers, the large and voracious-looking grille, the small side inlets of polished aluminium, the slightly rising bonnet, given greater elegance by its length. The dashboard is laid out in exactly the same way as the 250, and unfortunately the five central dials (including the clock at the extreme right) cannot conveniently be seen by the driver when the car is being driven fast.

The sound of the Spider's 240bhp is softer than that of the 280bhp of the 250, although the exhausts are identical. There is slightly less the sense of all hell being let loose as the rev-counter climbs. But all this is relative, of course. Once the power is engaged, the tyres start to spir before gripping the road surface and then hurling the car forward. In spite of its 40 fewer bhp, the California is still possessed of outstanding acceleration. At 7000 revs, first takes the Spider up to around 62mph and second to about the halfway mark on the speedometer: 93mph. After that, there seems no stopping the machine 125, 130... Only the winding road holds the needle of the speedometer back from travelling right round the dial. It is now that the slightly stiff but very precise gearbox comes into its own, although there is no point in pushing the car too far. The change from grear to gear is a bit on the slow side and road-holding on these tyres is well below the level needed to exploit the engine fully. Even without taking the car up to the speeds of which it is capable, driving the Spider still needs constant attention to stop it from spinning completely. The Dunlop '175' tyres, as I remarked above, are quite inadequate for the amount of power which is transmitted to the wheels. The two strong points of the car are the very powerful brakes (if they have been well adjusted) and the high precision ZF steering. I would have preferred a slightly smaller steering wheel because of the extreme lightness of the steering, but the fashion of the time was for large steering wheels, even when they were not necessary.

To call this car 'marvellous' would not be too strong a description; although it was first introduced as long ago as 1961, it still makes at least three-quarters of current automobile production look very inferior. The one area where it could have been improved (to make the driver's life a little easier) is its road-holding, which is only too reminiscent of the age in which it was first designed.

One shortcoming of the Spider I have forgotten to mention is that putting up the hood needs Herculean strength and patience, which is why most Spiders remain either hooded or open for life.

Beneath the bonnet was the powerful Ferrari engine, ready to hurl the car forward towards the horizon.

LU · 6508

Clothiers

JAGUAR

JAGUAR XK120

This Jaguar bears little relation to the sporting cars of today. Comfort and sufficient space were obviously not considered absolute necessities by its manufacturers and yet, in spite of this, the XK 120 remains a very attractive car. This creation with its tiny boot, the two narrow seats crammed between the rear axle and the huge bonnet sowed terror among the other roadsters of the time; and, indeed, it has remained the truest expression of the roadster to appear in the last thirty years.

The greatest attractions of the car were also, paradoxically, its main shortcomings: there was something very special about a quick trip from Paris to Deauville in one of those cramped seats. Beneath the disproportionately long bonnet, an engine of 160bhp. The car's steering, however, was very heavy and it lacked synchromesh on first gear. Even the most committed enthusiast would sometimes feel that there was a lack of virility in the car's appearance: it was certainly true that the XK 120 did have an obvious stylishness which was not to the liking of the adherents of brute force. However, a true roadster had to have a certain style, so that it never passed unnoticed.

The suspension of the XK 120 was never hard, which created considerable problems for a sporting car. The wheel clearance, and the flexibility of the torsion bars, were more like those found in a tourer. If the suspension was disappointing, so too was the engine.

At first sight, the twin overhead camshafts made this an attractive looking power unit, but the long stroke was a less fortunate feature; somehow, the power of the engine was diluted. The power was certainly there at the lower end of the rev range and the XK 120 could accelerate quite easily from 1000rpm in fourth, demonstrating the torque of the engine. There was a distinct lack of power, however, in the upper reaches of the rev scale which made acceleration at high speed difficult. Above 112mph, it was supposedly possible to move slowly and painfully up to 125mph, but the best we ever achieved in our test car was 116mph.

During our test drives, we found there was no problem with the handling of the XK 120 on motorways where the road surface was in perfect condition. But anyone who likes a challenge when driving would be very much at home in this car on bad surfaces. At 85mph and above, it started to move about all over the road and any driver would need to have a strong belief in his own luck to keep his foot down on the accelerator. If the front slid to the right, then there was hardly time to correct it before it was going towards the left. There was one golden rule in driving the XK 120 — always expect the unexpected — because if the unexpected ever happened, then there would be no point in anticipating any help from the brakes.

These were weak to the point of non-existence; in fact, if it was a question of braking late, there was usually no point in braking at all. A number of 120 owners, preferring effectiveness to authenticity, have replaced the drums with the discs which were later incorporated in the XK 150. These were much more powerful and fade-resistant.

Fewer difficulties attended the operation of the gearbox, although it did take some getting used to. For those purists who found that the entirely synchromesh boxes which became standard on all Jaguars after 1965 were not masculine enough, there was nothing more exciting in the XK 120 than double declutching at 25mph charge from second to first. Moving up through the gears also needed a double pedal movement if a strange cracking sound, as the gear engaged, was to be avoided. This feature was inseparable from the style of the 120 and, if it didn't provide the excitement of the old Bugatti direct-drive dog-clutch, a challenging difficulty was certainly there. At maximum revs of 5200, first took the speed to 37mph, second to 68mph and third to 100mph.

Once the driver has gained an accurate impression of the brakes and has learned how to use the gearbox, all that was necessary to learn how to corner in the XK 120. In this respect, the XK never appeared a difficult car to drive; indeed, because of its very precise steering, it could be positioned to within the nearest millimetre on long bends which could be taken without any problems at all. But, in direct proportion to the tightness of the bend, the weight of front end would take over, making the steering harder. On short bends, the lack of power to counteract understeer became noticeable. Over uneven and bumpy ground, the XK 120 had rather strange reactions, jumping and sliding and generally losing its grip on the surface. The lesson of all this is simply not to be too ambitious in the XK 120 in bends. The curious carriage-style bench seats put the driver's body at the mercy of centrifugal force. I mention lefthanded bends particularly, since the driver could use the door to maintain his own stability in right-handed bends, or vice versa for right-hand drive cars. For nearside bends, then, the steering wheel had to be considered as a kind of life-belt

The Jaguar XK 120's accommodation was mainly two seats, two doors and a dashboard with its dials grouped in the centre.

and the driver had to make sure that his hands did not slip on the leather.

The bench seats were surrounded by a fairly luxurious array of fittings; their leather was admirably set off by the floor carpet, which indicated that the XK 120 could claim descent from a limousine family.

The softness of the clutch pedal contrasted with the more brutal side of the engine, which tended to overheat in town. There was a certain uncivilized quality about the whole assembly, with the badly synchonized gearbox, the steering which was especially heavy when the car was stationary, the almost useless brakes and the engine which lost all flexibility at high revs.

Like the Bugatti, the XK 120 was a roadster full of paradoxes and almost seemed to have been made to produce deep divisions of opinion. In fact, the arguments between those for and those against the XK 120 only really came to an end with the appearance of the F-type. Although the mechanical parts — the engine and gearbox, at least — of the latter were virtually identical to those of the 120, the brilliance of its design and its marvellous flowing lines brought the

The XK 120'S narrow grille, long bonnet and two-part windscreen made it a favourite in the American sports car market of the fifties.

PASADENA
CALIFORNIA
13566
JIM RICKMAN MTRS.

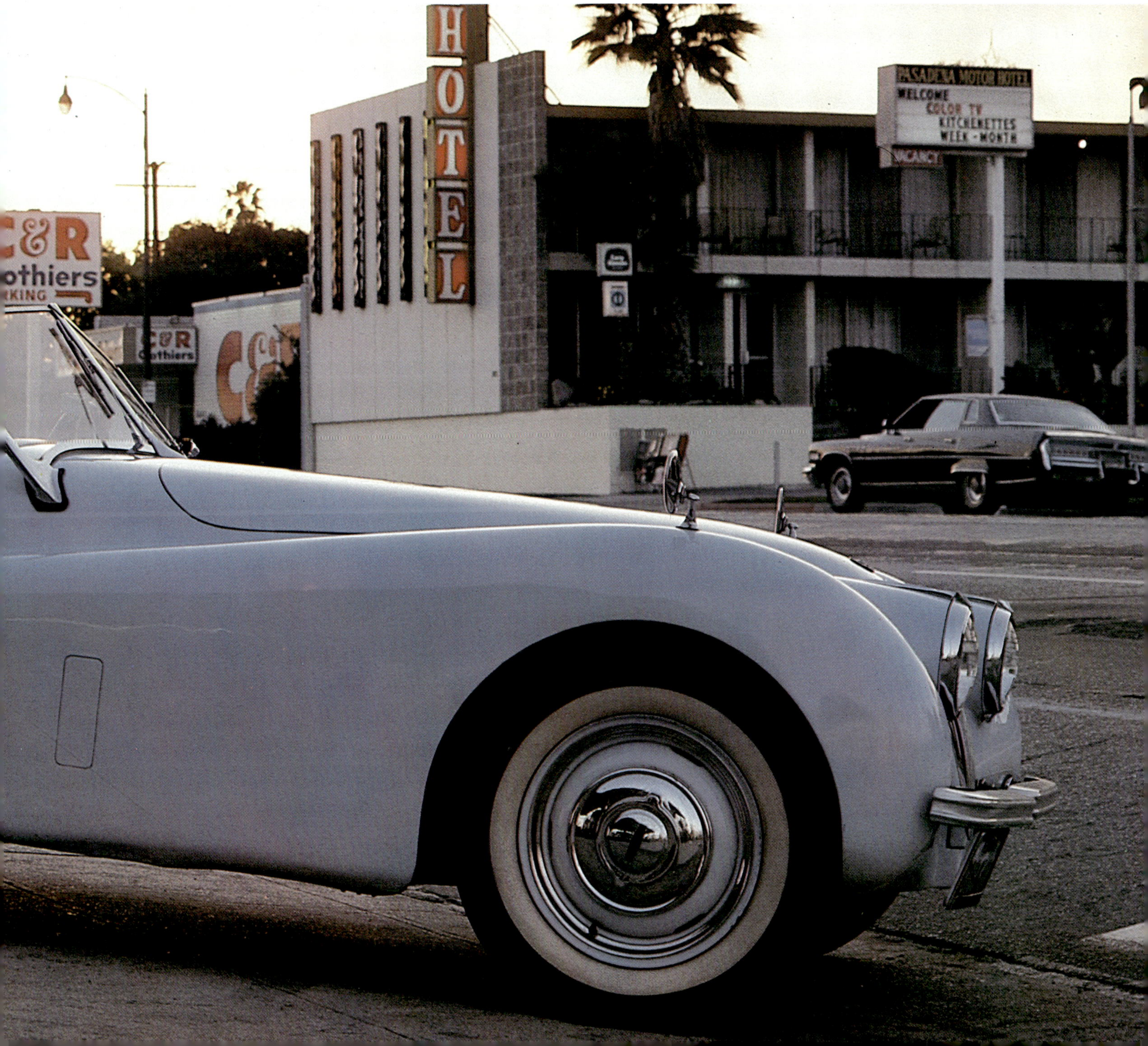

two arguing factions together. Unfortunately, between the 120 and the E-type came the 140 and the 150.

Jaguar enthusiasts managed to accept the XK 140, though with bad grace, since it still kept some of the sense of style of the 120. There were points to be regretted, though: the disappearance of the rear wheel spats, the over-heavy bumpers and the retention of the two-part windscreen. But the true devotees of the 120 must have felt quite sick at the appearance of the XK 150. Admittedly, the radiator grille had been made wider, but this was absolutely necessary for the cooling of the more powerful engine. The heavy bumpers were retained, but the two-part windscreen disappeared to be replaced by a larger, curved one which certainly displeased the purists. These latter tend to forget, however, that the engine was now worthy of the body. It was still a straight-six either of 3442cc developing 213bhp (SAE), or 3781cc developing 223bhp (SAE) or, even better, were the 3·4S or the 3·8S developing 253bhp and 268bhp, respectively. The gearbox, with its non-synchromesh first speed, not surprisingly, remained — meaning that the mechanical aspects of the car had not really evolved since the XK 120, apart from the introduction of the four disc brakes. The top of the 150 range was undoubtedly the XK 150S in its coupe version, that is, a hardtop two-seater.

Apart from this, there were great differences between the car of the early fifties and that of the late fifties. The XK 120 was a stylish, majestic car, with distinctive breeding, but it should logically have been equipped with a much more powerful and flexible engine from the beginning of the decade to put it on an equal footing with cars of equivalent engine size, such as the 300SL Mercedes. However, this was not to be and, in spite of this handicap, the 120 did manage to conquer the important American market which before the invasion of European sports cars of the fifties, had started to create its own — the Corvette and the Thunderbird — but that's another story.

E TYPE 3.8 litre

The Jaguar E-type was something else altogether: 269bhp instead of the 160 of the XK 120, and ten years between them. Inside were two bucket seats and a dashboard of milled aluminium carrying the minor dials.

The E-type was not a car which could ever be ignored! Even people who had never really looked at a car before were captivated by the long, low body and the fine lines of the bonnet and the sides, right down to the exhausts. Any passer-by, seeing the E-type parked by the pavement, so low that the seats would appear almost at ground level, could not fail to be stirred by the sight of the car. Even today, it is still exciting, although its narrow tyres, especially at the front, betray the age of the design.

Its engine was the direct descendant of that of the old XK 150. Our test model was in fact powered by the 3·8-litre XK engine with the non-synchro first gear. This engine developed 269bhp at 5500rpm. One curiosity was its long stroke, 106mm, against a bore of just 87mm. In practical terms, this meant lack of flexibility at higher revs, the engine producing disturbing vibrations above 5000rpm. The 3·8-litre models were produced from 1961 to 1964. There were twin chain-driven overhead camshafts and three HD8 horizontal SU carburettors.

The rear suspension was a marvel of ingenuity: independent by wishbones, radius arms, coil springs and dampers. The disc brakes were 'inboard', meaning they were close to the differential.

During the sixties, the E-type was the ideal sports car, or almost. It is easy to see why it was so popular; it was, after all, the near-relation of a very successful line of sports-racing cars. In many ways, it was unfortunate that the Jaguar engineers had to adapt it for the public road by softening the brutal aspects of the Le Mans D-type to make it a more civilized car. There was little brutality remaining in the E-type, marketed from 1961 onwards, or any insurmountable problems in driving it.

At between 5000 and 5300rpm, first produced 40mph, second 75mph, and third 103mph. Acceleration was not ultra-rapid, but the pressure transmitted through the bucket seat to the lower part of the back, and the sudden sensation of speed indicated that the E-type could travel very fast indeed. Up to 125-130mph, at about 5000rpm, there were no problems about the acceleration. Above that speed, acceleration was slow and there was noticeable engine vibration. In a hard-top version, less sought-after by collectors than the drophead coupé, I reached 139mph.

Acceleration trials gave the following results: standing 400 metres in 16·2 seconds; standing kilometre in 29·8 seconds; 0 to 100kph in 9·4 seconds. Since my test car had already done more than 60,000 miles, I decided not to take it above 5000rpm. To demonstrate the flexibility of the engine, the 400 metres took 18 seconds in fourth from 40kph and 32·4 seconds for the 1000 metres. All of which I would have expected from the powerful straight-six, giving 36mkg of torque at 4000rpm. In fact, so tractable was the engine, that it was possible to travel considerable distances without changing

WATER
OIL
FUEL
MAP
STARTER
PANEL
INTERIOR
FJDC

Superb lines, and an elegant bonnet under which was concealed a twin-cam straight-six fed by three SU carburettors. The gearbox had four forward speeds, with non-synchromesh first.

gear at all, just like a vulgar, low-bred limousine.

An easy car to drive, the E-type was a marvellous assembly of mechanical qualities, from the wishbone suspension to the light steering and the gear changing, except of course for the double declutching necessary to return to first. The noise of the exhaust was very discreet, perhaps too discreet. Personally, I would have preferred something harsher, more brutal, to go with the aggressive look of the car. One of the strong points of the E-type was its petrol consumption; as long as it was driven at moderate speed, no faster than 100mph, consumption would be in the region of 204 miles to the gallon (imp), which was quite remarkable for an engine of that size.

In spite of its undoubted high-performance features, the E-type had other, less impressive characteristics which became particularly noticeable when reaching the upper limits of its performance. Above 112mph its long, aggressive bonnet would start to move as the car lost its directional stability, especially if the road surface was not perfect. This movement would never reach very dangerous proportions and there was never any risk of serious danger, which one sometimes believed *was* possible with the XK 120. It was not, in any case, advisable, to hold the E-type too long at the limits of its performance. The designers had skimped somewhat on the grille which was just too narrow for the radiator to breathe properly. The same problem occurred on the 4·2-litre models. This anomaly was finally corrected in 1969, when the radiator grille was enlarged and two electric fans added. But a careful watch still had to be kept on the water temperature.

The weight of the E-type (1200kg) and the fact that there was a concentration of this over the front axle meant that steering could be quite a problem in tight bends, when the steering tended to get heavier and the direction of the front end to become very difficult to control. Long bends, however, produced exactly the opposite and the oversteer would be a major problem. The car needed to be set up for the bend very carefully and then planty of pressure applied to the accelerator; if this was not done carefully, then there was a very distinct tendency to slide, which could also happen if the driver was obliged to take his foot off the accelerator suddenly. In these circumstances, more direct steering would have helped, although the 2·75 turns from lock-to-lock should have been sufficient to avoid such worries. The steering was, in fact, precise and light, bearing in mind that a lot of the weight was over the front axle.

Like all the Jaguars, the E-type responded badly to powerful applications of the brakes, which also tended to have very little staying power. Although it was equipped with four perfectly good Girling discs, the E-type's brakes were virtually useless when overheated. A single lap at Monthléry would be enough to render them totally powerless; after ten kilometres, not only would the E-type not brake any more, but the whole assembly would start to jump and vibrate.

Made for the public road, and not for the racing circuit — unlike the D-type — the E-type never aspired to being a sports racing car, in spite of its undoubtedly racy appearance, which it really needed to captivate its potential owners and drivers. Indeed, its interior was quite luxurious and almost worthy of limousine finish. The dials were proudly displayed on an aluminium dashboard. The two leather seats recalled the comfort of English interiors, but they did support the back well.

An E-type was never expected to emit the same kind of roaring engine sound as a Ferrari, or to corner like a Grand Prix car, or climb like an Alpine Group 4. Its fine lines, and its easily achieved 125mph were quite enough to lift it well above the commonplace.

The E-type, then, was a worthy successor to the XK series of the fifties, retaining the 3·8 litre engine and the gearbox with non-synchromesh first gear. However, to complete the history of Jaguar sports cars from 1950 to 1965, I should now mention the model which followed the 3·8-litre. Fortunately, no changes were made to the styling (which was not the case with the horrors of the Series III and after), except for the appearance of '4·2' on the boot lid. However, there were two fundamental changes. The first concerned the gearbox, which received a synchromesh first gear in 1965, ending the era of double declutching. The second innovation was the introduction of a 4·2-litre engine, although this did not entail a great gain in power, which remained at 269bhp but at 100rpm less; the torque, however, increased from 35·95mkg to 39mkg at 4000rpm. The drophead version lost 40 kilos in weight and the hardtop 50. In more practical terms, the power weight ratio was now bhp/4·4 kg for the new coupé against 4·5 for the old.

These changes were quite far-reaching, although they may seem relatively insignificant on the surface. However, the Jaguar engineers, when making these modifications, should certainly have paid far more attention to improving the cooling system; equally certainly, they should never have changed the design of the head gasket which became extremely fragile after 1965.

Some enthusiasts prefer the E-type coupé, though the cabriolet, with its hood down, was very striking indeed. The beautiful, long bonnet was to be recognized as characterising this fabulously successful Jaguar for many years to come.

9751AL92

9751AL92

LANCIA

Opposite each other, the Lancia B 20 and the 2800 Zagato with its aluminium body. Beneath the bodies, the same efficiency in the engine and gearbox.

3563 UU 75

LANCIA AURELIA B 20

The Aurelia B20 is one of the great but forgotten cars of the fifties, despite its undoubted qualities. The Alfa-Romeos, the XK 120s of the period, all have their enthusiastic bands of followers and collectors, but the B20 seems to have disappeared into a sort of automobile limbo, when it would have merited being one of the most sought-after expressions of postwar car design.

It may be that its styling has something to do with this neglect. The lines are perhaps a little too restrained to excite those fifties collectors who prefer long, rakish bonnets. And the car is too recent for those who prefer the true vintage period. It did, however, have its own stylishness, which is much too easily forgotten today.

Admittedly, the engine was not the most brilliant piece of engineering, but it was sturdy and reliable. The six-cylinders were in V-form, with a twin choke carburettor; top revs were 5200, developing 118bhp. Although this does not compare very favourable with cars capable of really high performance per litre (118bhp for a 2·5-litres is very little), the Aurelia was far from being a sluggard: the standing kilometre in 34·4 seconds and 400 metres in 18·6 seconds. In 1958, such performance figures were as rare as psychedelic T-shirts. Up to 93mph, acceleration was easy and swift, but from there to the promised maximum of 114mph the lack of horsepower and an overdrive in fourth made themselves felt.

Our test car was equipped with a gearlever on the floor (option), although this had too long a movement between second and third. The box itself was rather sturdy, but it had one shortcoming which was unworthy of the car as a whole: a non-synchromesh first gear.

There was one curious, disconcerting aspect of the B20: the apparent lack of engine noise audible from the inside; it wasn't simply the absence of the deep growl of a powerful engine — there was no noise at all. After consultation with experts on the car it was concluded that all the noise went out through the twin exhausts. And indeed, it was only necessary to half-open the window to allow the deep notes of the exhaust into the car — so deep that one could easily have been in the middle of a fleet of Ferraris!

When I said that the B20 deserved much better at the hands of present-day enthusiasts, I based my remarks on the fact that this was basically a very sound car. It was especially well-balanced, the weight of the engine being countered by a De Dion *"Haute époque"* rear axle; the clutch, gearbox and brake system were also very well engineered.

The B20, then, was a car of considerable quality. One drawback, however, was the front suspension. This was by rigid axle, but with an adjustable hydraulic dumping system for the wheels. The whole system, however, tended to overheat and become softer as a result, necessitating frequent adjustements.

The Aurelia did, however, take longer bends very easily, holding the road well and without rolling or movement of either the front or rear ends; all four wheels firmly adhered to the road surface. These qualities were even more noticeable when it came to tackling winding roads. Firstly, the car remained very well balanced, with a suspicion of oversteer, if required by the driver. By and large, the independent suspension was quite capable of dealing with the problems posed by such roads, although there were occasionally slight losses of grip by the front wheels. Secondly the direct, precise steering, easy to manipulate in tight bends, was another great advantage once the car was set up for a bend. Thirdly, the drum brakes lost very little of their power, even after several miles of intensive use. Fourthly, the flexibility of the engine in third made rapid acceleration possible, and it was very easy to change down into second anyway, if needed. Lastly, the comfort of the ride remained very much at the level of a luxury limousine.

It is hard to offer any other conclusion to this test than to return to my opening theme: the Aurelia was forgotten too soon.

It is not surprising, though, that the B20 was capable of better performance than the majority of its competitors, especially if we examine the range of its components. The basic design was classic, with the engine in front, rearwheel-drive, gearbox on the axle; but there were also a number of technically interesting innovations. The engine was a 60-degree V6 of 2451cc, with a 78mm bore and a relatively long stroke of 85·5mm. This is why the maximum power of 118bhp was attainable at the relatively low engine speed of 5000rpm. There was nothing unusual about the torque at 18·5mkg at 3000rpm, while the compression ratio was never greater than 8:l. Since the engine was a V6, it was logical that the camshaft should be positioned in the centre of the vee. The carburettor was an efficient down-draught twin Weber. Transmission was by a four-speed gearbox (with a non-synchromesh first) positioned near the rear axle. The clutch was a single plate unit. In theory, the four wheels had independent

Small window area on the B 20, but very good road performance.

suspension, but this was not totally correct, since the two front wheels were linked by a rigid axle. However, there was an independent element in the leaf-springs, which were no doubt regarded as quite satisfactory at the time, despite the over-heating change problems.

The rear suspension was by a very up-to-date de Dion axle with semi-elliptic springs. The rear brakes were technically very advanced, and were rather like those of the Jaguar E-type. Both front and rear brakes were drums and worked very efficiently. Steering was worm and sector.

2800 ZAGATO

For most people nowadays the mention of the name Lancia conjures up one image: the superb performances of the Stratos in the gifted hands of the Italian Sandro Munari and the Frenchman Bernard Darniche who, in recording their many victories, put the name of Lancia (taken over by Fiat in 1960) at the top of European rallying in the seventies.

The dimensions of the B20 made it a well-proportioned car with a sensible wheelbase of 2·65m, which made for very good road-holding in bends. The front track was 1·28m, while the rear was slightly wider at 1·30m. Overall length was 4·37m, width 1·55m, and height 1·36m. The biggest drawback of the specifications was the weight of 1·150kg, dry and unladen. The original tyres were 165 × 400 on rims of 5 × 15.

Beneath its relatively sober exterior, then, the B20 was a well-engineered and comfortable car. It is to be hoped that the results of the test drive given here will make it a more popular car amongst enthusiasts.

The history of this old and well-established company had already been marked previously by a list of interesting innovations, which included the integral chassis of the Lambda in the twenties and, in the post-war years, a succession of powerful and successful sports cars. In the fifties Lancia introduced yet another car in this line of descent, the Aurelia, which also had a number of outstanding features for its time, including a powerful V6 engine, supremely efficient brakes and a four-speed gearbox attached to the De Dion rear axle. Altogether, a very impressive piece of engineering.

It was hardly surprising, then, that the successor to the B20 should take over some of its most attractive characteristics. This was the Flaminia, which was officially introduced in 1956, but only really began its active life after the Turin Motor Show of 1958 in a variety of bodies designed by the three great masters of the time: Pininfarina, Touring and

The 'Superleggera' was designed by Zagato. It weighed 1320kg.

Flaminia Super Sport
LANCIA
3563 UU 75

3563
UU 75
LANCIA

Zagato. Pininfarina offered a square-looking saloon with a 2·75 metre wheelbase and an overall weight of 1500 kg. There was also a heavy-looking coupé in the same style with an identical wheelbase and of comparable power : 140bhp (CUNA) — CUNA is an intermediate measurement between SAE and DIN and was used only by Italian manufacturers in the past.

The Touring version of the Flaminia used the shorter wheelbase of 2·52 m and was produced as a two-door GT coupé weighing 1360kg, a cabriolet of 1400 and a super-coupé of 1420cc. All these models were much lighter than those turned out by Pininfarina, thanks to the famous 'Superleggera' bodywork. But there is no doubt that the most beautiful version and the one which expressed the spirit of the car most accurately was that produced by Zagato.

A rapid résumé of the work of Zagato would probably concentrate on two aspects. The first is aesthetic: the lines are always fluid, the rear ends unfussy and the front ends closely allied to the technical needs of the chassis. The second strength is the light bodywork, generally of aluminium, as in the car tried here, a Flaminia 2800 Supersport with the short wheelbase and weighing a mere 1320kg, a record for such a large coupé (4·49m in length).

This elegant coupé was powered by a V6 engine, developing 152bhp at 5600rpm. Its maximum speed was 134mph.

Designed in 1963, with modifications to various details over the years, this car hardly appears to have aged at all. There is hardly a wrinkle in its appearance to contemporary eyes: no narrow track or old-fashioned bumpers. True, there may be some debate about the rather too-rectangular radiator grille or the unusual treatment of the headlamps, but very little else. Personally, I find it one of the most completely successful designs of the period.

The Flaminia Zagato was not, however, just a pretty plaything, to be seen and not touched. Its fine exterior hid some fery impressive engineering. Following the Lancia tradition, the body and chassis were integral and the engine and the whole of the front end were supported by an auxiliary chassis, which greatly facilitated construction and repair. The engine was a V6 of 2775cc (85 × 81·5mm) with overhead valves. A very important feature was the inclusion of a cylinder block and cylinder heads in light alloy. When equipped with three twin choke downdraught 40DCN 12 Weber carburettors, the engine developed 152bhp at 5600rpm.

The suspension was ultra-modern with wishbones and coil springs in front. The rear, however, was much more complex, incorporating a De Dion axle held by semi-elliptic springs and completed by an anti-roll har. Above this was a four-speed synchromesh gearbox attached to the differential, which helped to balance the weight between the front and back axle. From 1959 the Flaminia was equipped with four servo-assisted Dunlop disc brakes; the steering by recirculating balls was, however, a little old-fashioned.

In all styling and mechanical aspects, then, the Flaminia as conceived by Zagato was a very fine car: a marvellous combination of lightness and power. Nor were the details neglected: windscreen washer, two-speed wipers, separate front seats (not always standard in the fifties), trip-recorder, retractable headlamps, lighting in the engine compartment and boot. Clearly, it would have been possible to do without such refinements in a car which tended towards the sporting. But the skill of Zagato lay in giving the occupants of the car the impression of living dangerously, but in a setting of some luxury.

Although the gear ratios left something to be desired (third was too long), the combination of 152bhp and a weight of only 1300kg gave the car very rapid acceleration. The standing kilometre came in 31 seconds, a very respectable figure for an old, re-modelled V6. It took under II seconds to get from O to 60mph; first took us to 31, second to 68, and third to 108, with the needle finding its maximum at 134mph. Roadholding and directional stability were excellent, though the first touch of the brakes would almost send the driver through the windscreen, without any significant skidding.

There were some faults found in the Flaminia, although in almost all aspects this was the perfect car with an almost uniquely happy combination of mechanical and aesthetic features.

A sports or grand touring car usually has some major fault, either with the engine, the brakes, the steering or the gearbox. The Zagato 2800 was almost perfect in every aspect, although the gear changes were a little imprecise because of the controls needed for a box located at the rear. The steering was reasonably precise but probably geared down too far and direction became increasingly less controllable as the speed of the car rose.

These were minor criticisms, however, and the Zagato supersport 2800 remains a very attractive car with fine lines and highly efficient performance. I would personally criticize the dashboard as being too 'Italian' — rather overcomplicated in its layout with over-large and badly-positioned dials, but that is the total sum of my criticism of this great car.

11 FPAGB
DUNLOP SP

LOTUS

LOTUS SEVEN

At speed, the hood of the Lotus Seven was so tightly stretched by the pressure of air that it always looked as though it was about to rip. The draughts inside this primitive car seemed to start around the foot of the door, rise up by the driver's left hand and then carry on across his fingers, hands and arms. But the attention needed to keep the car on the road, especially on bad surfaces, was usually so great that the draught would eventually be relegated to the status of minor inconvenience although, to complete its progress, it would follow the body up to the neck and end its movement by blowing around the heads of the driver and his passenger.

Jammed between the vibrating door and the transmission tunnel, the driver would desperately try to make out the irregularities of the road through the mean little windscreen. At the slightest bump or hole, the Lotus would take off on one or two wheels and then fall back to the surface, slightly on the slant. There was certainly no possibility of trying to find out where the second current of air, blowing counter to the first, had come from. At speed, the noise in the car became almost intolerable: the flapping of the hood combined with cracking noises coming from the aluminium body. The bonnet vibrated terribly, while the wings, which looked as frail as those of a butterfly, trembled at every shock caused by the very hard suspension. A quiet and serious conversation between driver and passenger was an impossibility: at least three-quarters would have been lost in the noise.

Like the Morgan, the Lotus Seven was an extraordinary car, it was simple and primitive and sold in kit form during the first few years from 1957 to 1964. The Seven first appeared in 1957 powered by a pathetic 1172cc sidevalve engine taken from the contemporary small Ford saloon and developing a frightening 40bhp at 4500rpm. In 1964 the Series 2 made its appearance with either the Ford 105E or the Austin-Healey Sprite ohv engine. Later, around 1970, the Seven was given more power in the form of a 1600cc Twin Cam engine developing 118bhp at 6500rpm and there were other variations. Later, other engines were to be used, including a 2-litre unit, developing 140bhp, which turned the 600-kg Lotus into a kind of flying bomb.

The Lotus which was test-driven by us was one of the Series I cars, although certain parts of the body had been replaced by components from Series 2.

Essentially, then, this extraordinary contraption was powered, if that is the correct word, by an old-fashioned straight-four Ford sidevalve engine, with a long stroke of 92·5mm against a bore of 63·5mm, giving 1172cc. The maximum power obtainable from this unit was 40bhp at 4500rpm. The gearbox was a three-speed antiquity with a non-synchromesh first gear. The engine was located at the front end of a multi-tubular steel chassis, with independent suspension at the front and live axle at the rear with coil springs and Panhard rod. The four drum brakes were non-assisted. The supreme luxury of the car, though absolutely necessary to obtain even remotely respectable performances, was the aluminium body.

Given the fact that the Lotus Seven of that period weighed no more than 500kg, it would have been reasonable to expect rapid acceleration. We were very disappointed. The standing kilometre took 38 seconds. Another problem appeared at maximum speed on the circuit at Montlhéry where, after two laps at maximum speed, the temperature rose to 100° and it was therefore necessary to slow down. However, we did manage to reach the 'terrifying' speed of 88mph with the hood up. Although these figures are disappointing, it has to be remembered that the old-fashioned shape of the car, its almost non-existent aerodynamic qualities, its 1930-style wings and its prominent headlamps all made a high top speed unlikely.

The true home of the Lotus Seven was the race track or winding roads: never the motorway. Its major qualities lay in its steering, its handling and its relatively rapid pick-up of speed. On the other hand, the gearbox looked at first sight like an assembly of all possible faults: first non-synchromesh, second and third ratios too 'long'. However, the gate, was very precise, although the passage from one gear to another could be difficult. The steering was rack and pinion and acceptably direct, with three turns from lock-to-lock, making it possible to position the 500 kg of tubular steel and aluminium with great precision. In fact, one the great pleasures of driving this strange machine was to appreciate its sheer agility. It may seem absurd that it was possible to take pleasure in driving a machine with such an odd specification, but that was indeed the case.

It may seem just as strange to praise the handling qualities of the Lotus Seven and it is true that it did take a little time to fathom the mysteries of its performance. In fact, the tendency of the rear end to break away could be quickly rectified; only very tight bends brought out a

With its antiquated looks, the 1960 Lotus Seven harked back to the shape of pre-war cars.

tendency to understeer because of the lack of power. Planted four-square on its four wheels, the road-holding was excellent; in this respect the Lotus Seven demonstrated the genius of Colin Chapman and his supreme knowledge of racing and getting the best out of a car. So, in spite of its nervous disposition and low top speed, the 1960 model was really a very sensible car. It lacked power and disc brakes, but these were to be added later, making the Seven into a great toy for adults, as long as they could drive — and drive well!

The Lotus Seven is essentially the sort of car that everyone should own once in a lifetime, unless the desire for comfort and driving ease is strong. It was an elemental car, a constant battle to control, and yet, great fun to drive. A car providing the delight of heel and toeing in a machine expressly designed for it, and the perverse pleasure of sitting cramped in the narrow driving seat in one of the most primitively appointed postwar vehicles conceivable. Later, this character was to change somewhat with the introduction of more powerful engines and the improved gearbox. However, the Lotus Seven remains a great driving experience, although the words used to describe it may prove more tender than the reality!

A tiny cockpit, which was largely taken up by the transmission tunnel, made driving the Seven rather like driving a small Formula racing car. In front of the steering wheel, the wings and headlamps vibrated to the rhythm of the straight-four fed by two twin-choke carburettors.

LOTUS

The body of the Sebring GTIS was far from being elegant. This heavy car, with body designed by Vignale, could still reach 175mph thanks to its 235bhp.

SEBRING 3500 GTIS

At the beginning of the sixties, the firm of Maserati still enjoyed considerable prestige in the motoring world, principally due to its pre-war success on the race track. During the fifties, the company had tried to recapture some of its former glories in competition. But the apparent inability of the various models to gain suitable results finally led Maserati to concentrate on the production of the powerful grand tourers.

There was a certain amount of practical sense in this decision to change course, since the Modena company was desperately in need of saleable cars to assure its financial future. By 1965, then, the Maserati range was composed of a number of expensive, powerful and very elaborate models, all produced to challenge the pre-eminent position of Ferrari. The line of development of the successive Maseratis was sometimes a little strange, but the cars themselves were undoubtedly exceptional.

The basic model of the range was the 2+2 Sebring coupé, termed the 3500 GTIS, a beautiful but slightly old-fashioned design by Vignale. Then came the 'two' *Posti* in coupé or cabriolet forms and, at the top of the range, the terrifying Quattroporte and the monster 5000 GT developing 340bhp. This was massive power for a car of that period.

It was not enough for the company, however, simply to have a range of immensely powerful cars to sell; it also undertook considerable amounts of technical research, developing four separate engines, the least powerful of which gave 235bhp! These engines were employed in the various models of the range. First came the 3500 GTIS, the basic model, with its heavy yet stylish design, which was equipped with a dual-ignition straight-six, with twin camshafts and Lucas injection, of 3485cc, developing 235bhp. The 'two' Posti had a 3692cc version, developing 245bhp or, with some tuning and additions, 280bhp. The third engine, and certainly not the least, was that of the Quattroporte: a 90° V8 of 4136cc, giving 260bhp. The final power unit was the 40° V8 of the enormous 5-litre coupé with its 4941cc giving 340bhp.

I would have liked to try the whole range of Maserati engines as they were in 1965. What a joy they must have been at the time for engineers all round the world! But although the engines, the gearboxes and even the interiors of these cars were worthy of the best that Italy could produce, the rear suspensions were oddly old-fashioned. A rigid axle was fitted to all the models, which provided pitifully little stability for such power. The only exception to this was the Quattroporte which was fitted with a de Dion rear axle which was fixed to the chassis. The road-holding of the other Maseratis was seriously affected by the rear axle which provided no protection at all against the irregularities of the road above 125mph.

I chose the 3500 GTIS as test car, since it was the most representative and the most popular of the whole Maserati range. This was a large coupé, designed by Vignale, with a fairly heavy look about it. The top of the wings was positioned relatively high in relation to the body as a whole, while the sloping windscreen gave an impression of irresistible power. One aesthetic shortcoming was the square-styled rear end, which was much less attractive than the front end with its relatively fine lines. Some changes were made between the 1964 and 1965 models, including horizontal sidelights. The steel body rested on a tubular frame which provided the necessary rigidity to cope with the power of the engine. This latter aspect of the car was a real work of art and was certainly not to be entrusted to inexperienced hands. The stroke of the 3500cc straight-six was long: 100mm for a bore of 88mm. Thanks to the twin overhead camshafts and the Lucas indirect injection, the engine developed its 235bhp (DIN) at 5500rpm. The compression ratio was 8·8:l, and the torque 32mkg at 4000rpm.

Behind the source of all this power was positioned the famous ZF five-speed all-synchromesh gearbox. With an axle ratio of 3·769:l, the car's maximum speed was 146mph. It would hardly be possible to criticize the 3500 GTIS up to this point, except for some loss of road-holding ability on sub-standard surfaces. This was due mainly to the inability of the rear axle to deal with the power transmitted by such a large engine. The braking system, on the other hand, was well worthy of high performance motoring: four dual-circuit Girling disc brakes assisted by two servos! This was a virtually faultless system both in power and durability.

The ride and the interior comfort may have left little to be desired, but the road-holding certainly had to be looked at with considerable circumspection, if only because a 235bhp engine with limited flexibility needs very careful handling. In addition, the rear end tended to move about uncontrollably at speed if the driver was ever less than very sensitive with the accelerator or if the road surface was extremely bad, unless the car was equipped with an anti-roll bar, which

Flat grille, double headlights — the Sebring looked a very powerful car.

was a rare addition at the time. Altogether, driving a 3500 was a question of delicate judgement, especially in controlling the power in relation to the shortcomings of the rear suspension. The ZF gearbox also needed special attention in use, if only because of a certain stiffness in the synchromesh. The ratios, however, were admirably matched and the fourth gear gave 125mph on the speedometer.

Closer examination of the steering revealed many unfortunate aspects which have to be put down to its relative obsolescence. The Burman recirculating ball system was simply not very precise. But considerable improvements were to come in 1965, making the car much easier to control and eliminating that steering inacurracy which could send cold shivers down the driver's spine. The diameter of the steering wheel was large, in accordance with the style of the time but not much help in critical situations.

It remains only to describe the magnificent dashboard even though the latter had certain shortcomings which are well known to connoisseurs of the 3500 GTIS. However, it is fair to say that it would be unlikely for so many demands to be made on the car's instruments that these shortcomings would become evident. What was evident was the attractive layout, with the main dials very visibly grouped together and the remainder of the controls positioned on the central console. There was also a grab handle for the passenger.

MERCEDES

300 SL MERCEDES

There have been very few cars which have had such larger-than-life qualities as the 300 SL and have become so surrounded by myth and legend. Certainly, the reputation of one of the most famous of all postwar sports cars had already spread far and wide by 1954. There were good reasons for this fame: the 300 SL had everything, it was simultaneously a dream car, a racing car and a sports car. Its performance could rival those of present-day Ferraris and Maseratis. In 1955, even Aston Martin and Jaguar had to admit their inferiority to a car which could go from 0 to 60mph in around 7 seconds — no other manufacturer could even have dreamt of such figures at the time. The remarkable flexibility and power of the engine gave the 300 SL its amazing acceleration, which was just as effective at Le Mans as during a country drive. Altogether, it was a formidable but carefully judged mixture of brutality and finesse.

Facing the driver were two huge dials which were raised slightly above the main part of the dashboard; these were the speedometer, calibrated to 168mph, and the rev-counter with a danger zone beginning at 6000rpm. The oil pressure gauge and the clock completed the instrumentation, which was largely sufficient for this car.

Once the gullwing doors had been closed, the cockpit of the 300 SL could feel a little cramped. The window surface, especially at the front of the car, was rather narrow in comparison with modern cars. Beyond the windscreen could be seen the rounded curves of the front wings, and above that was the narrow band of visibility in which could be seen the road. After reassuring himself that his view of the outside world was actually sufficient, the driver could finally put the 300 SL in motion. The clutch pedal was stiff, but there was no problem with the gearchanges. However, once the wheels started to turn, a heaviness and stiffness in the steering could be felt, as though all the weight concentrated in the front end of the car was just a little too much for it. Anyway, steering was certainly two-handed work.

The ferociousness of the engine soon became apparent, as the driver moved through the gears, and the noise would increase to a point where it would have been easy to believe there were twelve-cylinders under the bonnet. Up to 4000rpm this effect was not so noticeable, but afterwards the full orchestra of the engine could be heard. The noise diminished slightly when gearchanges were made at 6000rpm, only to regain its strength and intensity after the top ratio had been engaged.

If you have to test a 300SL now, however, never make the mistake of thinking that all these characteristics can be studied at your ease. In spite of being twenty-eight years old, a 300 SL will still leave you hardly the time to breathe. In the car belonging to the Bec-Hellouin Museum, we reached 60mph in 7 seconds and did the standing kilometre in 27·4 seconds — figures which would almost make a present-day 500 SEC green with envy.

The 3-litre direct injection engine developed 245bhp (SAE) at 6100rpm; acceleration to round about 120mph (5000-5500rpm) was effortless. It then took a short while to reach 6000rpm which brought 140mph on the speedometer. We reached 133mph on the motorway with this car which has a production model final drive ratio of 3·64:1. During the production period there were optional ratios of 3·42 : 1 or 3·25 :1 which gave such cars maximum speeds of 156mph or more. But the majority of the 300 SL were delivered with the 3·64 :1, which allowed a very high top speed and very good acceleration.

The Mercedes 300 SL: a car with brutish power. Gullwing doors and an aluminium body for this version of the car, of which only 29 were built.

Developing 81bhp to the litre, the engine of the SL had tractability equal to American production engines. Its impressive power at low revs meant that it could loiter in fourth at 1000rpm without problem. This was one of the great advantages of the car: imagine driving at 25mph, the gullwing doors open, trying to pick up a girl on the Champs-Elysées at four in the afternoon. It was almost as if the designers at Mercedes had taken this important Parisian problem into account when they built the car!

The suspension, however, was a wholly serious matter and treated as such. The independent front suspension

300 SL
CH
SG
2019

In the aluminium version, the straight-six, direct injection engine gave 240bhp; the production model gave 215bhp. Apart from the Rudge wheels, the two models were identical in appearance.

MERCEDES
BENZ

CH
SG
2019

was by wishbones, coil springs, dampers and anti-roll bar; rear suspension was by swing axles, coil springs and dampers. This system made the SL a very sure-footed car on the road; on the motorway its handling was impeccable, even at maximum speed. Indeed, it was on the road, whether in good or bad conditions, that one could truly appreciate the qualities of this car: its sureness, balance and overall quality.

At first, the speed and acceleration can cause anxiety, then you suddenly realize that you are taking bends at a speed which would cause a lesser car to leave the road at a very early stage of the journey. Medium and long bends could be taken with no problems at all. The 300 SL would cling to the road marvellously, then its precise steering would correct the line without the driver needing to lift his foot from the accelerator. There was, however, one small shortcoming in this catalogue of brilliant features: the brakes. It was certainly regrettable that our test model was not fitted with the discs which made their appearance on the 300 SL cabriolets in 1961. The earlier models, like out test car, were fitted with drum brakes, which were just about adequate; or, at least, so they appeared in 1982. But the effort on the pedal needed to make them work efficiently somewhat spoilt the feel of all-conquering efficiency which the SL had given up to that point. The operation of the brakes did, however, provide a marvellous opportunity for strenuous exercise of the driver's right leg.

The front end of the SL was obviously very heavy and was therefore hardly made for taking tight bends easily. However, in these circumstances the power of the engine was very useful. An experienced driver would set up the car sideways for the bend and then slide through it, still maintaining pressure on the accelerator. the precise steering then made it a simple matter to correct the direction and any good driver could make a very good impression in a 300 SL on a winding circuit. There were no complaints about the gearbox, although the synchromesh was a little slow, and the ratios were well able to cope with any conditions: first, 44mph; second, 75mph; third, 106mph.

The level of comfort inside left no doubt as to what kind of car the 300 SL was intended to be. No concession was made to delicate spinal columns or to lovers of soft upholstery; it was more or less tolerable according to the state of the road and the degree of security expected in such a car. Nevertheless, it could subject its occupants to some very sharp and brutal experiences. The air-conditioning was very effective, thus compensating for the lack of opening windows. The car did, however, lack even the most rudimentary side pockets.

Summing up the total effect of the SL

Two large dials, a two-spoked steering wheel and a gearlever to control the four synchromesh gears.

is not hard. Apart from its very hard brakes and a few shortcomings like restricted visibility, the 300 SL could easily be a contemporary car and would compare extremely favourably with most current production models. Many so-called sports cars now in production would, of course, be totally humiliated in the comparison. One drive in the SL would convince most people of this...

There is another dimension to the 300 SL story: the creation of the special 300 SL for rallying, which was the true successor to the 300 SLR. This was a car of extraordinary quality and very exciting. The body was made entirely of aluminium, taking 200kg off the weight of the production 300 SL. The engine, developing 240bhp (DIN), was 25bhp more powerful than that of the production model. This increase in power was made possible by modifications to the cylinder head and camshaft. The acceleration of the rally model was quite astonishing and, although the top speed was hardly different from that of the production cars, it could now be reached in just 24 seconds. The rest of the car was no different, except for the Rudge-hubbed wheels which theoretically distinguished the specials from the classic 300 SL.

300 S

The history of Mercedes is a story of powerful cars' — sporting cabriolets and outright racing cars, the most famous of which would easily bear comparison with the pre-war Auto Unions. During the period from 1930 to 1940, the company produced a spectacular range of sumptuous coupés and cabriolets, of which the most celebrated were the 500K and the 540K, in other words, the supercharged 5 and 5·4-litres models.

After World War II, production had to recommence in very different economic circumstances with very different purchasing powers. Gone were the great cars and super-luxury cabriolets which were to be seen in Monte Carlo and Beverly Hills. Yet the change was perhaps not as great as might have been expected; the real expertise of Mercedes lay in the production of luxury cars, which were both speedy and expensive. The introduction of the 300 in the autumn of 1951, then, was not such a surprise. This was a beautifully proportioned limousine, powered by a straightsix developing 115bhp. From this essentially town car came, in 1952, a two-seater (or 2+2) cabriolet which had the same general styling as the 300 and was logically designated the 300 S. It had the same power unit as the 300 but with twin carburettors; it developed 150bhp to give a maximum speed of 100mph. The price in Britain at that time was £5,530.

The lines of the new Mercedes had a certain heaviness, yet the 300 S did give an impression of power. Its styling, in fact, had a distinct resemblance to the supercharged Mercedes of the pre-war period. There was the familiar massive snout, enveloping wings and large hood which covered an appreciable amount of the car. In many ways, it represented a direct continuation of the traditional style of the company, very much at home in the production of luxury cars. Developing its 150bhp at 5200rpm, the engine had plenty of power — just right for doing the journey from Paris to Marseilles at one go in style and comfort. The major defect of the car were its relatively inefficient drum brakes which also lacked durability. The weight of the 300 S was a substantial 1680kg, or 20kg heavier than the limousine.

A few minor modifications were introduced in 1954, mainly to the mechanical parts of the car, which made the 300 S cabriolet, now mechanically identical to the limousine, a true masterpiece of an automobile, or at least almost!

In 1954, the year which saw the introduction of the truly sporting 300 SL, the 300 S had its power increased to 165bhp at 5000rpm, which was still relatively low considering the modern design of the engine. This was still a 3-litre unit or, more precisely, 2996cc. It was a straight-six with overhead valves and camshaft but, instead of twin carburettors, it had a down-draught type Solex 40 PBJC. Maximum torque now increased from 22·5 to 24·7mkg at 3900rpm. In fact, this was the same power unit which was to be installed in the mighty 300 SL where its power would be increased to 245bhp, thanks to Bosch direct fuel injection.

The 300 S, however, was far from achieving such performance figures. At 165bhp, though still powerful, this car could hardly have sporting pretensions. Any element of its styling which suggested sportiness was only really disguising its almost limousine qualities; it was essentially a car for people who no longer required violent sensations. Nevertheless, the basic engineering was of such high quality that it was used for the 300 SL and it would be hard to pay a higher compliment to any power unit.

The gearbox was a four-speed all synchromesh unit with the lever on the steering column (it was direct from the

The 300 S cabriolet was the logical successor to the 500 and 540 of the forties. Massive front end, well-appointed dashboard and a pre-war style radiator grille.

box in the 300 SI); the final drive ratio was 4·67:I. The differential assembly of the rear axle was extremely complex. The rear suspension was by half swing axles and coil springs with auxiliary coil springs. Unlike the 300 saloon, however, the 300 S did not have the disengageable additional springs on the torsion bars (fitted in the saloon to take any extra load) as it was thought that the cabriolet would not be called upon to carry heavy loads.

The front suspension was independent by wishbones and coil springs; there was also an anti-roll bar to help cornering, so well equipped was this Mercedes. The brakes of the 300 S were judged inadequate when the model was first introduced; in 1954, however, it was fitted with 'turbo-effect' drum brakes, by which cold air was played over the drums

if they became overheated and lost efficiency. The same device was applied to the brakes of the 300 SL but was to prove quite inadequate for that model. As far as the 300 S was concerned, the mechanism did take a load off the driver's right foot! The steering was typical of Mercedes-Benz, precise and very direct, with three turns from lock-to-lock.

In describing the mechanical attributes of the 300 S, there is a danger of missing its true quality, which was really expressed in its interior. So well fitted was the 300 S, that it is hard to arrive at a description which will do it full justice. After taking in the chrome surround of the windscreen, the eyes would light upon the beautifully finished dashboard of solid walnut and encrusted with various chromed gadgets including the speedometer, the clock, and the powerfull radio (with valves). There was also a variety of push-buttons for the diversion of the driver and the control of mechanical parts.

The steering wheel was of the usual large diameter of the time and featured a duplicate interior circle, of chrome, for the control of the horn.

Once the driver had engaged first gear, the smoothness of the engine, with its noiseless pushrods and pistons, would carry the occupants of the 300 S towards an unforgettable experience. The four ratios never had to be pushed to their limits; all that had to be done was 1-2-3-4 and 165bhp was ready under the driver's foot to answer his slightest whim. The great willingness of these 'horses' helped by an almost magic amount of torque; fourth gear would pick up from 1000rpm, almost as if some magic fluid had been injected to create a sixteen-cylinder engine of 20-litres.

The noise of the engine hardly rose when the accelerator was pressed. The comfort of the car was in no way disturbed, remaining an ideal marriage between perfect suspension and soft and deep leather seats which were so comfortable they could have been taken for water beds. More aggressive acceleration could push the body down on its soft suspension a bit, producing some understeer, which was only to be expected, since the front end was very heavy. But in fact, the road-holding of the 300 S was extremely good. If there was any untoward sliding to disturb the tranquillity of the ride, this could easily be corrected by the light, precise steering. The brakes fitted to the later models were quite worthy of this extremely dignified car; the system worked progressively and was resistant to over-heating. All this, of course, is said in the context of relatively modest speeds, since it would have been very wrong to maltreat the old 7·10 × 15 tyres which had to carry 1800kg as well as the well-dressed occupants of the car! And who then would have worried about the massive petrol consumption?

In spite of its sedate appearance, the 300 S was capable of moving very rapidly, thanks to 165bhp; the four drum brakes were 'turbo' cooled.

MGA

After the disappearance of the MG TF, which had retained many of the stylistic and performance features of the pre-war sports car, a replacement had to be found. This famous British company then brought out a rather hybrid model. The bodywork seemed to have been inspired by that of the Jaguar XK, but its performance was far below that of its nearest rival, the Triumph TR.

Our test car, driven one cold morning, was a 1959 model. In short, it was a two-seater roadster with a unitary steel body chassis. Rear suspension was by live axle, and front suspension was independent. The 1·588cc engine developed a pitiful 80bhp at 5500rpm. With torque of 12mkg at 3800rpm and a compression ratio of 8·1:1. The engine was a straight-four pushrod ohv, producing the following performance figures: 100mph top speed; standing 400 metres in 20 seconds; standing kilometre in 37·4 seconds. The company tried to improve this performance by introducing a more sporting MGA, with four disc brakes and a four-cylinder twin-cam engine, but this power unit was so badly engineered that models in which it was fitted regularly broke down. In fact, the record of the Twin Cam was so bad that the company was forced to introduce a new power unit in 1961 which was less ambitious, but still more powerful than the 1959 model in developing 93bhp. In addition, disc brakes were fitted to the front wheels.

In spite of these improvements, the MGA was still far from rivalling the performance of the TR3 A, which was a more responsive, virile and faster car.

For these reasons, I felt less than enthusiastic when I came to try out the test car and I expected the worst from the drive. The car itself, however, was in superb condition, having been completely restored to a very standard, even down to the wing seams, proving that the wings had been removed to be repainted separately. The wire wheels were in perfect condition and fitted with new Dunlop tyres. The seats were covered with green leather, while the carpet was beige. I must confess to a great surprise in seeing the condition of this car, since I had expected something very different!

The owner of this particular model was also extremely kind and helpful, particularly since his car was for sale and yet he was still prepared to let two strangers try it. Usually, when we borrow carefully restored cars, the owner issues a long list of dos and don'ts, drawing attention to the synchromesh, the paintwork which has been so painstakingly done that a disaster would provoke a nervous breakdown, and so on. The only comment offered here, as the owner gave me the keys, was that the car in question was not totally original.

Personally, I could see nothing out of place — no bloated wings or over-wide wheel rims. In fact, the gearbox, engine and overdrive had all been taken from an MGB. The engine had also been tuned by means of a Stage 3 kit, giving a high compression cylinder head (II:I), rallye-style camshaft and twin SU carburettors. The moving parts of the engine had been lightened and the unit developed a more acceptable 115bhp.

Comforted by these details about the hidden aspects of this gentle-looking car, I took my place in the driving seat and immediately felt as though I where sitting below the level of the pavement. The black steering wheel seemed immense, with a very thin rim. However, all the vital components seemed to be in their due place: the gearlever within reach, the instruments perfectly visible, including the petrol gauge which was positioned towards the right. This arrangement of instruments is worth noting, since the most important parts of the instrumentation tend to be hidden in more recent cars by the hands of the driver or by the steering wheel. The rev-counter was graduated to 5500rpm and there was a watching speedometer and another dial includes water temperature and oil pressure. The side pockets are in the doors. The radio and loudspeaker complete the arrangement of the dashboard.

The deep sounds from the exhaust make a pleasing cacophony of noise and power is available as soon as the accelerator is pressed. The driver was always fully conscious of the smallest details of driving an MGA, cramped between the steering wheel and the short gearlever. Acceleration is surprisingly rapid and 112mph comes up rapidly on the motorway; the standing 400 metres comes in 18 seconds (without use of the overdrive), while the standing kilometre takes 34·4 seconds. At high speed, the front end has a slight tendency to wander; but this movement is only slight and tends to happen when the road is rutted. There is, however, a lot of wind noise when the car is going faster than 62mph, at which point all conversation becomes impossible. This is, of course, a compliment, since a true British roadster *must* inflict draughts and cold on its occupants.

A number of features became more marked on minor roads. Road-holding, for instance, was extremely good, in spite of the new but old-fashioned Dunlop tyres. Acceleration was progressive, while the easy but imprecise steering

The little MGA looked attractive from every angle with its graceful back end and slightly streamlined front.

18 BP 93
DUNLOP

Narrow cockpit behind a relatively flat bonnet. The dashboard was kept to essentials.

provided a strong temptation to use opposite lock. I do not know whether the car would behave as well on damp surfaces, but given the narrow tyres, it would probably be very unwise to accelerate too suddenly. The ride provided by the suspension system (leaf springs rear and coil springs front) is quite acceptable and a far cry from the bumpy ride of the TR3. On the other hand, the steering column transmitted extremely strong vibration on bad surfaces — almost a sensation of holding an overactive sub-machine gun. Indeed, you have to remember to lift your foot occasionally if you want to return with your fingers and wrists still intact. These sensations are totally absent on good surfaces.

I would have expected well positioned pedals in such a car, so that it would have been easy to carry out heel and toeing. But no, we have to believe that the British have very splayed toes, which allow them to carry out this manœuvre without knocking their legs against the steering wheel and while still being able to operate the brake and accelerator at the same time!

In addition to its good performance, there were two other aspects of this modified MGA which pleased me: the gearbox and the brakes. The former had four forward speeds, with a non-synchromesh first. The lever was short and easy to move even though the changes were quite stiff, which meant that it was hard to use the engine to full advantage.

The discs and drum brakes were marvellous, servo assistance being available at no extra cost. The car could be slowed very quickly without any loss of direction. The system was also extremely durable.

If the MG had been fitted with a larger power unit at the time, the TR3 would never have enjoyed the success it did, while even the XK would have had a rival. In conclusion, it should be said that the remarkable condition of our test car made it a pleasure to drive in modern traffic conditions.

The engine of this car was that of the later MGB and gave 115bhp instead of the 80bhp of the 1958 MGA. The profile of the MGA made it look somewhat like a lighter version of the Jaguar XK 120.

LUCAS

MORGAN

TOURER+4

It is sometimes a mistake to want to relive the past, even the recent past. I have driven several Morgan Plus Fours and Plus Eights and I have found this a totally seductive experience at the time. The charm of these cars, I believe, is in their old-fashioned, but still very exciting styling. Their suspension systems were so hard and crude that a short trip of 100 miles felt like a military assault course. There were also the terrible draughts, obliging the hardened occupants to dress in high-altitude protective clothing. All these inconveniences, which had their own unique charm, put the Morgans in a very special category.

The Morgan is an institution. Its body was originally designed in 1936 and has hardly changed to this day.

Faced with the prospect of driving a Morgan again, my fond memories of the past would be subjected to critical examination. What had seemed charming then may have a very different aspect today. In any case, I now had an obligation to look at the car and test it as objectively as possible.

The body of the Morgan has not changed significantly since 1936. Today, there are three types of Morgan: the 1600 Plus Four roadster (two seater), the 1600 Plus Four tourer (four seater) and the 3500 Plus Eight roadster, with a top speed of 125mph.

I would have very much liked to have given some account of the Plus Eight with its indecently large engine and rapid acceleration for such a small car. However, I finally preferred its gentler predecessor, the nevertheless memorable Plus Four tourer.

Technically speaking, the Morgan dates from the thirties. Apart from its modern engine, the time-honoured method of manufacture is still used and the whole car is assembled by hand. The chassis is made up of a box frame with an X-form transverse supports, leaving something to be desired from the point of view of the car's overall rigidity. Amazingly, the front suspension system goes right back to 1910. It consists of vertical sliding pillars with coil springs and numerous bronze rings. This outmoded assembly needs careful lubrication every 300 miles (this is controlled by a button located beneath the dashboard). Rear suspension is by rigid axle (plus a 25 per cent limited-slip differential on the Plus Eight), semi-elliptic leaf springs and dampers. On this framework is placed the sheet-metal body which still has some supports made of wood. However,

7326UQ75

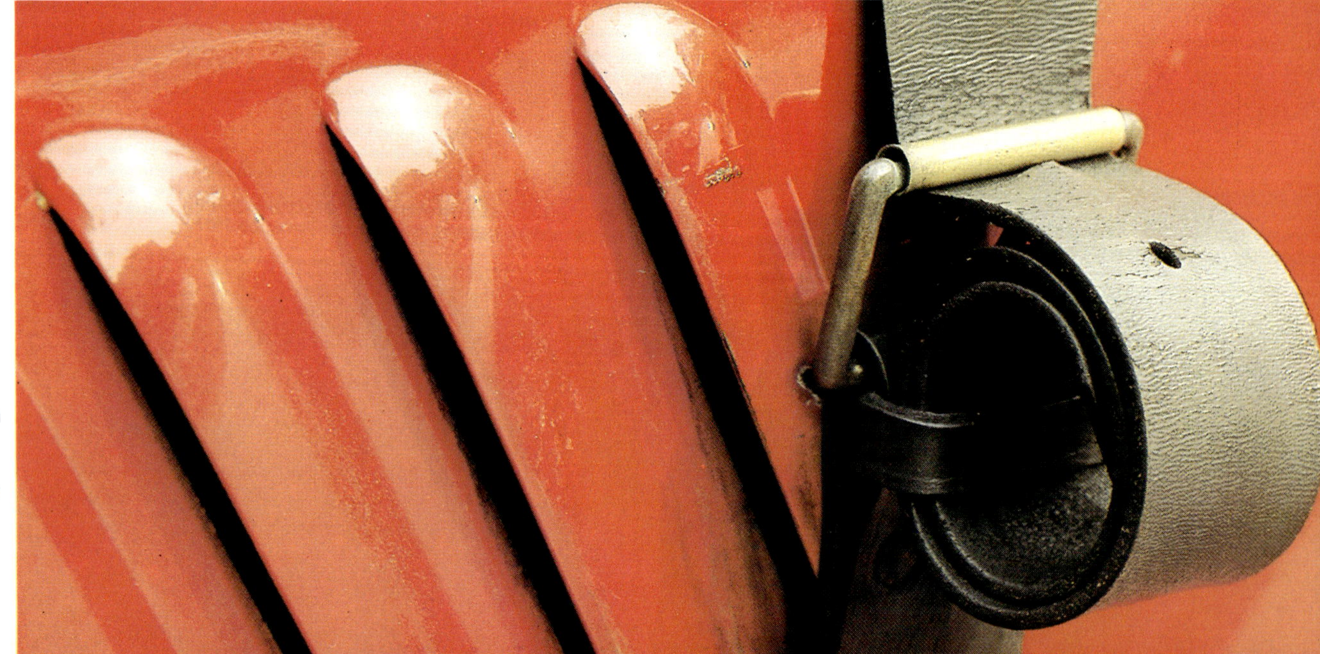

The Plus Four was powered by a 106bhp Triumph TR4 type engine. The Tourer was a four-seater. It features an elegant steering wheel, wooden dashboard and leather seats.

this small car (3·66m in length) weighs only 865kg in the tourer version (four seater), in spite of the weight of the TR4 A type engine. This is a straight-four of 2138cc, developing a respectable 106bhp at 4750rpm. The compression ratio is 9:1, and the torque 17·8mkg at 3350rpm. The crankshaft has three bearings. Fuel supply is by twin, horizontal, Stromberg carburettors. Transmission is a four-speed 'Moss' gearbox with non-synchromesh first. Steering is by worm and peg. The brakes are mixed: discs front, drums rear.

To be sure of remaining warm enough, the passengers and driver should really dress themselves very carefully from head to foot: hat, gloves, scarf wrapped ad least eight times round the neck, winter coat and airman's goggles to protect the eyes against cinders when driving close to the railway! These preparations are necessary whether the hood is up or not. At all but the lowest speeds, every part of the car is subject to strong currents of cold air, which affect eyes and arms and finally the whole body. When it rains, there are naturally leaks which are virtually impossible to stop. In fact, if you ever feel the temptation to buy a Morgan, there are only two things to do: either buy it immediately, or go and live in a warm country first.

Once the Plus Four gets under way, the hard, unforgiving suspension soon lets you know exactly what kind of ride you can expect. The slightest variation in the road surface is immediately communicated to the occupants and the inside comfort is very rudimentary, in spite of relatively flexible seats. Acceleration is very acceptable, thanks to a good power weight ratio and well matched gears. Limiting the engine to 5000rpm, the standing kilometre comes in 35·3 seconds, a very respectable figure given the inadequate CX ˎ tyres. Still at 5000rpm, first goes to 37mph, second to 62mph and third to 86. There is a slight delay before the maximum speed of 106mph comes up. At this point, it feels as though a gale is blowing through the car, although the road adhesion is impeccable. The noise is now that of a tropical storm, sweeping everything before it. The face of your passenger is clenched in a grimace so tight that it makes him virtually unrecognizable. And, of course, there is never a radio in a Morgan!

Test driving this Plus Four tourer reminds me of the one I used to own. This was bought several years ago in France; it had the same engine, was the same colour and made the remarkable average speed of 86mph from Tours to Paris. I remember passing over a tin in the road and being thrust into the air, my upward flight being stopped only by the hood. By the time I got to Paris, I realized I had lost one of the lever arm-type rear shock absorbers!

If the major criticism concerns the the almost non-existent comfort of the Morgan, the second concerns the gearbox. This is the 3·8 Jaguar gearbox, with its stiff gearchanges, non-synchromesh first and too much travel from 1 to 2 to make rapid acceleration possible. However, the precision of the gate and the ratios are perfect.

The steering is a little disappointing, especially when compared to that of the Triumph. It is not precise, direct nor easy to handle, and becomes noticeably worse at speed. The over-large steering wheel does not help, since the seats cannot be slid back very far, but force of circumstances soon teaches the driver how to handle this problem, by folding his arms close to his side.

The braking and road-holding have to be judged in the same way. As long as the road surface is very good, any tendency of the back to move around can be corrected by a light touch on the wheel and more power. But if the going is rough, then the loss of grip on the part of both rear and front ends forces the driver to develop a special, but risky, technique to cope with them. Movement of the body often gives the opposite impression to what is actually happening, thus what

The two rear seats were little more than symbolic. The engine, with its twin SU carburettors, was easily accessible thanks to a traditional split bonnet. Without its hood, the Tourer had very pleasing proportions.

looks like understeer is sometimes the opposite; also, if the car is being driven at speed, then, you never know whether it is going to oversteer or understeer — a strange dilemma! And a very rare phenomenon.

The efficiency and power of the brakes are not in doubt, although the lack of assistance is regrettable. However, if one or two wheels have lost their grip, hard braking will send the car skidding all over the place.

But perhaps it is unfair to judge a Morgan in these terms. For a Morgan enthusiast, everything is good in this car. If it is judged by someone expecting smooth, carefree rides, then clearly this is not the car for them.

However, I will terminate on a note of criticism. The Morgan's small radiator

tends to cause over-heating in traffic jams. There is a clear-cut remedy for this — or rather two. The area of the radiator grille should be increased and a supplementary fan placed in front of the radiator; if really necessary, an expansion tank can be added.

PORSCHE

356 A SPEEDSTER

Although this Porsche had a certain aesthetic strangeness, with its rounded curves which all seemed to be flowing into the ground, I must confess to a strong affection for it. Its design is derived directly from that of the Beetle, which is hardly surprising, since the same designer was responsible for both: Mr. Porsche. There was hardly a straight line in the design of the 356 — just rounded curves which gave the design very pure lines and good aerodynamics. There was still a stylized softness about the design,however, which seemed to date from pre-war years and which had already been rejected by numerous manufacturers by 1950. The long, flat front end of the 356 had more than just a suggestion of the 1930s *'Streamlined Moderne'* about it. But, old-fashioned or not, it did make for very efficient aerodynamics.

Contrary to what is often believed about this Porsche, there was nothing revolutionary about the chassis. This was punt-type of steel and derived directly from the VW, with similar front and rear suspension systems. These had been adjusted slightly but, though strong, remained seriously inadequate, especially in the case of the driven wheels. It is not necessary to be a genius to see the road-holding problems which could come from such swing axle arrangement.

Externally, though, the Porsche 356 looked sporting enough. The body was so low and the field of vision so narrow, that the driver often had the impression that he was lying on a mattress capable of moving at 125mph.

In an Aston Martin or a 300 SL the driver was seated more or less normally behind the bonnet. Stepping into the 356, however, was like entering a capsule which had been almost embedded in the ground. However, if the hopeful driver expected to find a world of engineering marvels underneath the car, he would have been very disappointed, for beneath the Speedster was the unmistakable lower region of the *Kubelwagen*.

Unless a test car is being pushed through a programme of very high, and illegal, speeds, there is nowadays little point in discussing road-holding and directional stability as all modern cars have good stability. However, at the period under discussion in this book, which was not so very long ago, this was far from being the case. The Speedster was very much of its time and up to a speed of 93mph, the front end would wander, but this was nothing serious. At higher speeds, and on the bad roads which are to be found in eastern California, the driver's attention had to be completely concentrated. On such surfaces the car would start to pitch as the front end suddenly became lighter and the front end would move from side to side. The Speedster rarely suffered from understeer; with all the weight behind and nothing in front, it was almost bound to oversteer, aided considerably by the easy, light steering. In both tight, right-angle bends and longer ones, the rear end would slide comfortably and safely. But if the driver had the misfortune to turn the steering wheel too violently or set the car up too soon for the bend, there was a danger of the outside wheel passing from negative camber to super-positive camber with results, which can easily be imagined, in the form of spectacular skids and spinning detrimental to the cardiac condition of the car's occupants.

Another speciality of the Speedster would become apparent in long bends, especially if they were being taken at speed. The car would be just holding its line, when the driver would find it necessary to lift his foot suddenly, perhaps because the bend had suddenly become tighter; in a tenth of a second the rear would swing about without warning and the driver would immediately have to switch over to the opposite lock. The moral of this story is that the driver of a Speedster had to be very sensitive to the needs of the steering and have lightning reflexes!

By 1956, a very good engine had been introduced; this was the 1498cc Porsche Carrera. (The name of 'Carrera' came from the trans-American race in which Porsche had recorded a class victory). The engine was the result of careful development work at Porsche and marked the serious beginnings of the company as a producer of sports cars. A flat-four, with block and cylinder heads of light alloy, four overhead camshafts, and developing 100bhp at 6200rpm this was a beautifully engineered power unit and gave off a very satisfying sound.

Unfortunately, my test car did not have the Carrera engine. However, perhaps that was all for the good, since I was a little anxious about having 100bhp so close to the rear bumper which had a disconcerting tendency to want to swap places with the front bumper. I therefore had to cope with the classic flatfour in its modified 1582cc version: 75bhp at 5500rpm, twin camshafts and one Solex carburettor per bank of cylinders. The whole was far cooled with a small oil radiator. Compression ratio was 8·2:1.

The engine took up little space, but was so tightly positioned in its compartment that repairs were a considerable

The Porsche 356 A was strictly a two-seater, unlike the 356 cabriolet.

problem. The whole assembly was located in an overhang behind the rear wheels, as in a Beetle. The differential was part of a transaxle with four entirely synchromesh gears; a rare luxury at the time.

However, the synchromesh did not work perfectly and it was often better to double declutch. The gearlever itself was very high and the gate tended to be rather imprecise.

But let us not be too critical. In general the operation of the gearbox was effective, clean and precise. The ratios corresponded well with the horsepower: 31mph in first, 56 in second and 84 in third. These ratios produced a very acceptable rate of acceleration, bringing up the standing 400 metres in 17.6 seconds, the standing kilometre in 35 seconds and the 0 to 60mph in just over 11 seconds — although this did not compare very well with a Carrera.

Nevertheless, the Super 90 engine managed to propel the squat body of the 356 with some conviction, even if it did tend to run out of steam towards 90mph. It was then that the driver would dream of a V12. And, indeed, the maximum speed was no more than 105mph which was still an experience to be reckoned with, since the Speedster at that speed could cause more anxiety than other cars at 140mph...

Although the suspension system was somewhat dated, the ride comfort was still considerable. The movements of the car were very easy on the body — fortunately, to counter-balance the stiffness and thinness of the seats, whose Germanic origins were very evident (even the seats of the 1982 models are still extremely uncomfortable).

The more I have examined the bodywork and styling of the Speedster, the more I have found it to have a troubling likeness to an overturned soup spoon! Inside, there is plenty of leg room, but the seats are positioned very low — or the doors are too high! Whatever the reason, I always have the impression that I have dived into a bathtub. And since the driver can see neither the front nor rear ends of the car, his sense of well-being is much greater than in a more conventional design.

It was another story, however, if the Speedster had to be driven with the hood up. This produced a sensation similar to the one experienced by a small boy trying on his grandfather's cap, which would then fall over his ears. The view in front became a matter of guesswork. At the same time, though, this feeling of being shut in was the perfect reflection of that generation of motor cars which the British described contemptuously as 'roadsters'.

In conclusion, it should not be forgotten that, significantly, this roadster also called the Speedster was to give birth to one of the most fabulous cars of postwar years: the modern Porsche.

A very low body with very flowing lines, gave an exciting, streamlined effect. The engine was an air-cooled flatfour, developing 75bhp. Note the basic dashboard.

PORSCHE 356 C

Each sports car has its own individual merits and faults. The merits are for the enthusiasts; the faults are for the professional critics. What is certain is that no sports car has ever excited a unanimous body of opinion. Speak of a Porsche with a connoisseur of Ferraris, and you might as well be talking to a brick wall.

Perhaps more than any other, the Porsche is a difficult car to understand. Made to be driven fast, yet the idea of putting virtually everything in the rear end will provoke endless debate. In describing the next car, then, I shall keep very much to my own personal opinions, allowing other drivers to judge it according to the performance and satisfaction they expect to find in such a sharply individualized automobile.

The 356C was the last of the Porsche 356 series which had started production in Switzerland in 1949, developing into the 356A in 1955, the 356B in 1959, and finally the C from 1963 to 1965, in September. By the time the C was introduced, the 356 range consisted of three models: the coupé, the cabriolet and the hardtop cabriolet. The styling of the body had obviously evolved since the introduction of the first models, but Ferry Porsche and his engineers carried out their modifications very slowly and gradually and never really touched the essential character of the car. This policy of gradual change made it possible to develop a well-balanced car, which had almost reached perfection by the time it was decided to withdraw it from production. And even now, the idea of continuity between models which are improved gradually, without bothering about what other makes are doing, is still one of the rigorously applied philosophies of the company.

Fifteen years after the introduction of the first 356, then, the body still retained roughly the same shape — a rounded shell, steeply inclined nose and fastback-style rear end. Obviously, the two-part windscreen had disappeared, as had the integrated bumpers and the huge wheels. But the classic lines were still there, and anyone faced with a 1950 356 and the C model would instantly recognize the family relationship.

In comparison to the aesthetic side, however, the mechanical aspects evolved more quickly. The first engine, for example, was almost that of the VW, developing 40bhp at 4000rpm. Similarly, the front suspension had the VW's transverse torsion bars. However, as the marque gained confidence, changes began to appear every year. The Carrera was introduced in 1962 with a 2-litre engine equipped with four camshafts and developing an astonishing 140bhp and when equipped with a Sebring silencer, the 356 Carrera was brutish — but a brute to warm the heart of every Porsche fanatic. In 1965, the Carrera 2000 GS engine still existed, but production models were equipped with a 1582cc versions.

From 1963 to 1965, in fact, two engines were available. For the coupé and hardtop 1600C there was a flat-four developing 75bhp at 5200rpm. The second engine was the 1600C for the cabriolet, also a flat-four, but developing 95bhp at 5800rpm.

The two engines had practically the same design. Bore was 82·5 mm with a

stroke of 74 mm. Although the power output was reasonable, the torque was not: 12·5mkg at 3600rpm for the 75bhp, and 12·6mkg at 4200rpm for the 95bhp. Fuel feed for the former was by two twin Zenith 32 NDIX carburettors, and for the 95bhp by two Solex 40 PJJ-4 twin-choke downdraught units. The engines were aircooled by means of a fan by an oil cooler which contained 5 litres. The clutch was a single plate unit, while the four-speed gearbox was entirely syncromesh.

The chassis of the Porsche 356 was integrated with the body. At first sight, the front suspension system looked rather archaic, although it had undergone many modifications since the first 356 models. It was independent by trailing arms and transverse torsion bars; the rear suspension was by swinging axles, radius arms and transverse torsion bars, not forgetting a huge anti-roll bar. The braking changed considerably in 1964, when the drums were replaced by discs — Dunlop ATE type — on all four wheels: these were not servo assisted. Steering was by worm and peg.

Event in its final version, the Porsche 356C still retained the traditional and simple dashboard which had always been free from unnecessary decoration and gadgets. Three principal dials faced the driver, with a small clock right in the centre. There was a grab handle for the passenger. From outside the car the interior gave the impression that it must

The 356 C, the last of the 356 series built from 1963 to 1965.

be rather cramped, but — in front at least — was actually quite spacious. This spaciousness was partly an illusion created by the absence of any protrusions from engine or gearbox; although there was some interference in the front space from the wheel housings, causing the driver to swing his legs to the right (left-hand drive models).

As was the case with many Porsche models, the action of the gearlever was relatively imprecise, finding the right gear and engaging it took a long time to master. Changing down, especially, created problems, since the driver had to grope around for the correct gear in the very imprecise gate. In my opinion, however, the greatest shortcoming of the 356C was its extreme sensitivity to cross winds and any irregularities in the road surface. Fast driving needed all the driver's concentration to hold a straight line by constant movement of the steering wheel. Fortunately, the actual comfort of the ride was very great, but this effect was certainly obtained at the expense of other capabilities, such as stability and road-holding.

Evidence that this was the case could be found in the tendency of the 356 to oversteer. This was not an altogether unpleasant sensation, since the tail sliding was progressive and never especially sudden. These reactions could be provoked by the driver and then simply corrected by use of the accelerator and steering wheel, which was easy and precise. My criticism here would be the ease with which the rear end would move off line, which could be uncomfortable and quite awkward if the road was in especially bad condition. It was, however, at very high speed and in long bends that the driver really had to show his skill: oversteer could happen very quickly in such circumstances. However all this was part of the real excitement of having a 356 to drive, of dominating the power of the car. It didn't really matter that there was very little torque, the only things that counted were the constant manipulation of the gearbox, the power of the ATE brakes (fitted to all four wheels in 1964, giving greater efficiency and durability) and remaining in command of a chassis with a mind of its own.

The 356C finally ceased production in September 1965. In 1966 the 912 appeared, a car whose modern lines differed very strongly from the outmoded looking 356. But the true Porsche enthusiasts regretted the passing of the old model and it took them a very long time to welcome the new. Modified over the years, the 912 became the 911 and 930: familiar forms among contemporary cars, cementing Porsche's reputation for fine cars through the years.

The double rear grille was a familiar feature of both the 356 C and SC. A well arranged and complete dashboard. The engine of the C developed 75bhp, with 95bhp for the SC.

TALBOT

The large 4·5-litre engine of the Talbot-Lago developed 210bhp, but this old-fashioned looking car weighed 1700kg! The dashboard was elegant in appearance with good instrumentation which was barely visible because of the four spokes of the steering wheel.

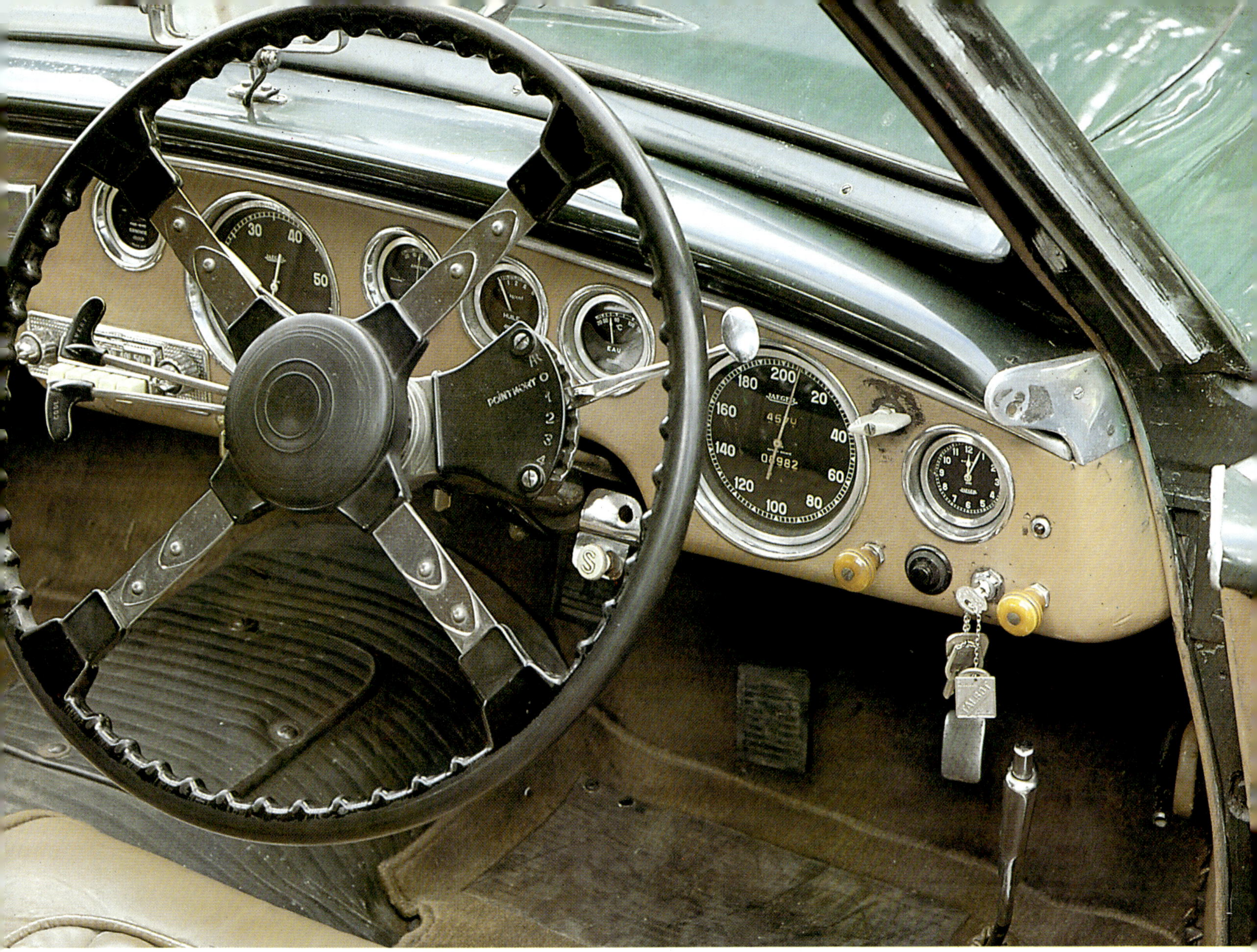
POINT MORT
JAEGER

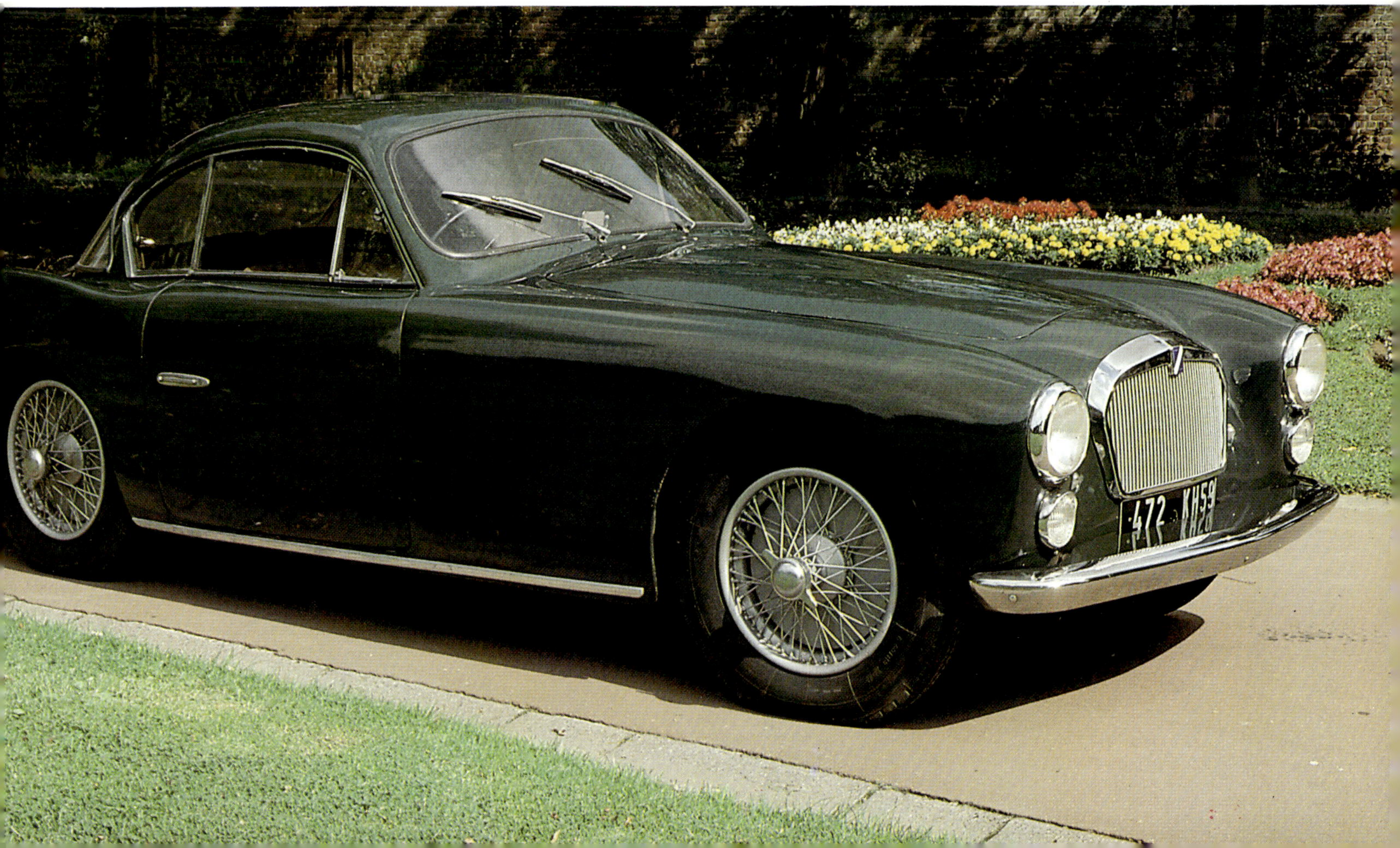
472 KH59

4.5 litre COUPE

There was nothing understated in lines of the 4·5-litre Talbot-Lago. Indeed, its styling was the quintessence of power and strength: this was the classic big car of the fifties.

In 1955, however, Talbot was obviously in a different class than Ferrari and Mercedes and made no pretence of rivalling them. At the beginning of the 1950s, however, Talbot had defended French motoring reputation against the claims of Italians and Anglo-Saxons with some success. Louis Rosier won at Le Mans in 1950 after driving throughout the race, except for two laps! Another Talbot, driven by Levegh, led the 1952 race for 23 hours, but was forced to retire one hour before the finish.

Talbot, then, was one of the last great independent French marques; a select band which had already lost Delahaye.

Two distinct problems immediately faced a driver on getting into this Talbot: the handbrake and steering wheel — the former was badly positioned and the latter over-large. Although the instrumentation on the dashboard was very complete, the actual positioning of the dials left a lot to be desired. Very little commonsense seems to have been applied when the dashboard was designed: the speedometer was totally unreadable, since it was hidden by the gearlever. At the other end of the dashboard, to the right of the steering column, was the rev counter, which was also virtually impossible to see without ocular gymnastics since it was partly hidden by the steering wheel. Only the oil, amp and water gauges fell within the natural field of view of the driver.

The engine flattered to deceive, with its twin camshafts. In reality, it was classic six-cylinder with pushrods and overhead valves in V-form. The cubic capacity was 4·5-litres and the unit developed a very respectable 210bhp. Transmission was via a Wilson gearbox with four semi-automatic speeds controlled by a preselector. When the driver had decided which gear he required, he placed the preselector in the gear above the one already engaged, or below if he wanted to change down: at the moment when the gear was needed, whether three seconds or ten minutes later, he could engage it by simply pressing on the clutch pedal. The advantage of this system was that it freed the driver from having to make sudden movements to change gears when he needed all his attention to be on the road, when taking a bend, for instance.

However ageless the front of the 4·5-litre Talbot-Lago may have looked, the tapering wings of the rear end place it firmly in its period.

The system did, however, take some getting used to. It was hard to remember at first that another gear could be taken without operating the clutch pedal at first; it was then necessary to press very hard on the pedal when the gear was required, otherwise the change would not happen and the pedal would snap back sharply against the foot of the driver.

Another drawback was the amount of heat generated; waves of excess heat would pass upwards from the gearbox and waft gradually around all the parts of the driver's body, until even opening the windows was no longer enough to get rid of the suffocating heat in the interior. The actual functioning of this gearbox, with its epicyclic trains, was very quiet, and the changes of speed happened easily, without any jerks. First took the car to 41mph, second to 65, third to 90.

A Jaguar XK weighed 1300 kilos and an Aston Martin DB2/4 1280; in contrast, the Talbot's chassis with bulky side-rails, and the weighty body, gave it an on the road weight of 1700 kilos, making it one of the heaviest cars of the time. It would have been normal, then, for its rate of acceleration to be very modest. However, once a certain amount of pressure had been exerted on the accelerator, the car would surge forward

very satisfactorily. The age of the test car didn't seem to matter in this respect and the performance of the engine soon dispelled any doubts I may have had. Any residual anxiety was totally set to rest by the very sporting noises from the exhaust. In strict mathematical terms, the Talbot could cover the standing kilometre in 33·2 seconds.

Up to 4000rpm the engine displayed plenty of tractability but, above that speed, it would start to give off rather alarming vibrations due to its long stroke. The only cure for this was to ease pressure on the accelerator at 4200rpm, which was usually reckoned to be the optimum engine speed. The above performance figures were achieved with a high axle ratio (2.92:1) model. The maximum speed was obviously affected by this and established itself at IIImph at 4300rpm. Overall the flexibility of the engine was not very impressive for 4·5-litres, and there were no real power until the revs had climbed to 2500:25mph took 35 seconds.

The great cast-iron engine, carefully positioned behind the front axle, and the imposing Wilson gearbox, which was placed in the centre of the car, gave the Talbot remarkable handling qualities, well in excess of any competitor. With a natural tendency to oversteer, though not excessive, the Talbot was easy to control. The only drawback in this respect was the relatively imprecise steering. The front did not feel too heavy in tight bends and the 210bhp could quickly get the 1700kg back into line, or at least on smooth surfaces.

If the road surface was bad, then the Talbot did have a tendency to wander, often without any warning. This loss of stability in such conditions was due to the imprecise steering, which took quite a lot of time to master. I did, however, note two points in its favour: it was light and the actual action of the wheel direct, with 2·75-turns from lock-to-lock.

The brakes were efficient enough to bring the Talbot to a halt without any loss of balance but, unfortunately, the four drums were prone to fade: although large, they were still not strong enough to stand up to the treatment meted out by the momentum of 1700kg.

The Talbot suffered from not having a modern chassis, which would have lightened the car. Its petrol consumption was much too high, as was its price. But it did have great solidity. When the Talbot company finally disappeared, it represented the end of the great French grand tourers.

1298 GK 92

TRIUMPH

TRIUMPH TR3

The grille of the TR3 spoke of aggression and its interior was almost less comfortable than a wheelbarrow. However, for the newly awakened younger generations of the sixties, the TR3 was the rebels' car. It belonged to the same era as neon lighting, black slip-on shoes and *West Side Story* in vistavision. Obviously, it lacked the class of an XK120 which managed to mix some aristocratic qualities with its aggressiveness. In France, the TR3 received the greatest accolade possible when one was bought by Johnny Halliday early in his career.

If the TR3 represented the middle range of roadsters, it was also the one which made the fewest concessions to the timorous and retiring: draughts,

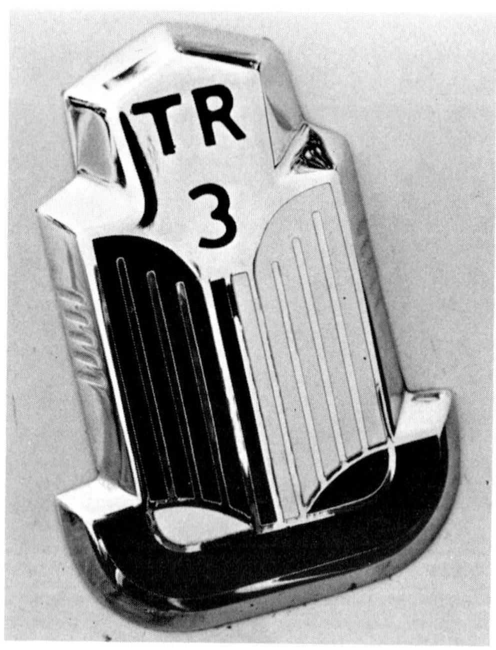

heavy controls and rudimentary comfort all came as standard. This was the essence of its character and the freedom it seemed to represent. The specifications were straightforward: 3·83m long, 100bhp and 940kg. These statistics were fleshed out by cutaway doors, a well-equipped instrument panel and bucket seats. Anyone possessing a car with such characteristics was usually looked on as partly delinquent or just the spoilt son or daughter of an over-indulgent father.

The mechanical side of the car was simple. The chassis incorporated two heavy box-type side rails and the engine was a classic long-stroke, four-cylinder of 1991cc. This unit was equipped with two semi-downdraught carburettors giving, for a compression ratio of 8·5:l, 100bhp at 5000rpm. There was nothing exceptional in a power ratio of 50·4bhp/litre, but the engine was tough and provided torque of 16·2mkg at 3000rpm. Moving rearwards from the engine, there was a single plate clutch, a four-speed gearbox with non-synchromesh first gear and optional overdrive on second, third and fourth. Rear suspension was by live axle, leaf springs and dampers; front suspension was independant by coil springs, wishbones and dampers.

The four Girling brakes comprised discs in front and drums at the rear. The steering was of the recirculating ball type. Other details were a 55-litre petrol tank, 58 AH battery and 155 x 15 tyres. All this added up to a very pleasurable, though basic, car.

The TR3 was strictly a two-seater. The bench behind made up for the limited boot space but was a terrible place for draughts; below was a 'secret' compartment for the spare wheel. Everything within the interior was designed to fit in limited space and to allow the execution of essential movements; there was certainly no room to let a pen fall or even to sneeze ...

There were six instruments, including a rev-counter calibrated to 6000 rpm, petrol, ammeter, oil pressure and water temperature gauges. The overdrive control was on the instrument panel to the left of the steering wheel and the hand brake was to the right of the transmission tunnel. One eccentricity was that the driver had to depress the button at the end of the handbrake lever when locking it into place; disengagement was accomplished by the driver pulling the brake lever towards him. This system had been installed to help the racing drivers at Le Mans, because it was imagined that it would be easier to operate than the classic system.

In 1958, the performance of the TR3 brilliant; nowadays, they look rather mediocre. Without using the overdrive, I covered the standing kilometre in 35·4 seconds, the 400 metres in 19 seconds. With overdrive, the figures were 37 and 20 respectively. Although these figures are no better than those realizable by many of today's family cars, they are still quite impressive. The feeling of speed is increased by the deep noise from the exaust, and the Spartan conditions which give the occupants a strong feeling of living very dangerously.

These figures show, however, that there was little point in using the overdrive on the middle gears; the torque was sufficiently high to do whithout it and the manipulation of the overdrive lever wasted time. It was useful with fourth gear, bringing the revs down by 500 and reducing petrol consumption.

The Triumph TR3, perhaps the best known and most attractive roadster ever?

Drivers who enjoy manipulating gearboxes had seven ratios at their disposal first, 34mph; second, 50mph; second overdrive, 62mph; third, 78mph; third overdrive, 90mph; fourth, 100mph; fourth overdrive, 108 mph the maximum speed I could achieve, although the speedometer registered an optimistic 124mph! The matching of gear ratios was perfect, though the changes were very stiff.

There were, however, persistant problems with the brakes; although these were powerful, durable and effective, the pedal demanded excessive pressure, as did the clutch pedal. The steering was very heavy indeed, especially when the car was stationary. Once in motion, this effort was reduced and, because of its great precision and directness, with 2 1/2 turns from lock to lock, the steering became acceptable. I was especially appreciative of the steering in bends, which the TR3 took extremely well. In normal driving, the car would hold its line well; at high speed a progressive oversteer would appear, although always controllable. The cars handling was good on well maintained road surfaces but a rapid deterioration in road-holding could take place on bad roads, with the car skating all over the surface. Tight bends would be marked by excessive understeer.

'Comfort' was almost non-existent in the TR3. If the going was easy, the inflexible suspension was hard, but just about tolerable. In any other conditions the occupants had to have recourse to their personal stamina and forget any inborn sense they may have had of gracious living.

If I seem to have painted a black picture of the TR3, it is because this description is of a true roadster. Enthusiasts will tell you that what looks like drawbacks are really great advantages and attractions.

The TR3 was amply provided with instruments and gears, of which there were seven: four normal and overdrive on second, third and fourth. Opposite: the TR3 at speed, with tonneau.

Achevé d'imprimer
sur les presses de Berger-Levrault à Nancy
en septembre 1983
Dépôt légal : 3e trimestre 1983
Imprimé en France